ESTATE PUBL

GLOUCESTERSHIRE

Street maps with index
Administrative Districts
Population Gazetteer
Road Map with index

Street plans prepared and published by ESTATE PUBLICATIONS, Bridewell House, TENTERDEN, KENT, and based upon the ORDNANCE SURVEY mapping with the permission of The Controller of H. M. Stationery Office.

The Publishers acknowledge the co-operation of the local authorities of towns represented in this atlas.

Estate Publications 479 B   ISBN 0 86084 799 3   © Crown Copyright 398713

COUNTY RED BOOK

GLOUCESTERSHIRE

contains street maps for each town centre

SUPER & LOCAL RED BOOKS

are street atlases with comprehensive local coverage

GLOUCESTER & CHELTENHAM

including: Bishops Cleeve, Brockworth, Hardwicke, Quedgeley, Shurdington, Upton St. Leonards etc.

STROUD & NAILSWORTH

including: Cam, Dursley Minchinhampton, Painswick, Stonehouse, Tetbury etc.

CONTENTS

LEGEND TO STREET PLANS

One-way street	→	Post Office	●
Pedestrianized	▨	Public Convenience	Ⓒ
Car Park	℗	Place of worship	✝

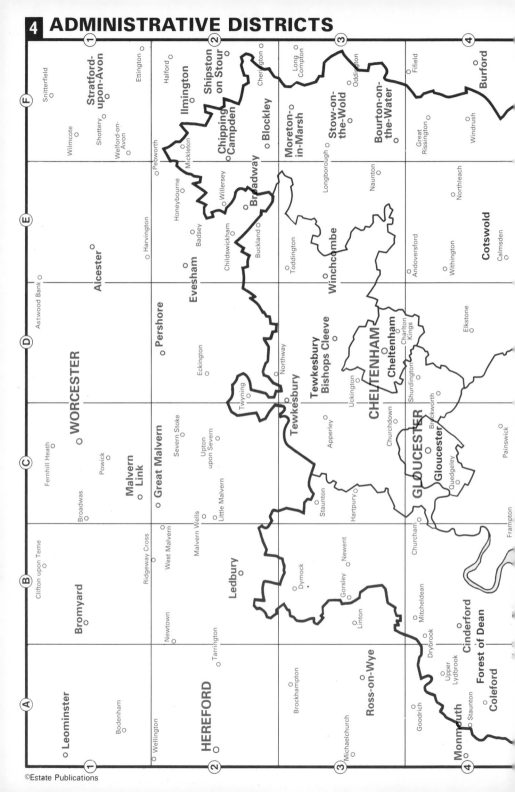

4 ADMINISTRATIVE DISTRICTS

©Estate Publications

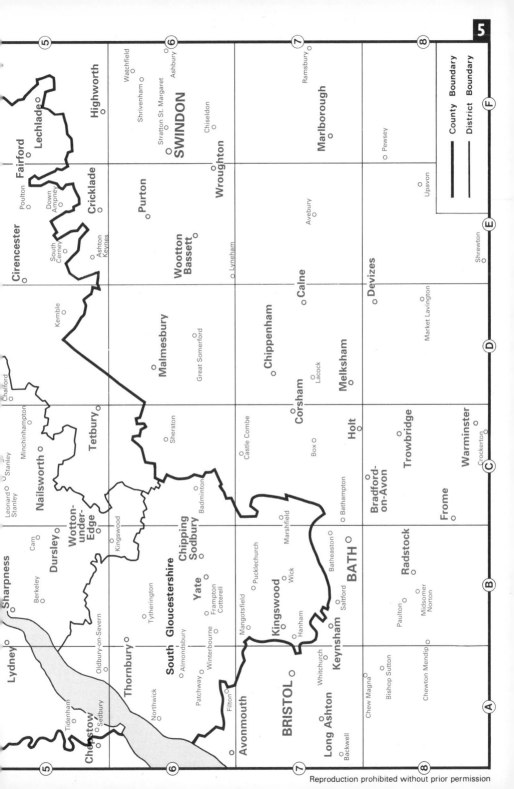

GAZETTEER INDEX TO ROAD MAP
with Populations

County of Gloucestershire population **748,734**

Districts:
Cheltenham **103,115**
Cotswold **73,965**
Forest of Dean **75,351**
Gloucester **101,608**
Kingswood **89,717**
Northavon **130,647**
Stroud **103,622**
Tewkesbury **70,709**

Ablington	11 H5
Acton Turville	11 E8
Adlestrop **127**	10 K3
Alderley **72**	9 D7
Alderton **681**	10 G2
Aldsworth **233**	11 J5
Alkington **641**	*
Almondsbury **7,317**	9 B8
Alstone	10 G3
Alveston **3,060**	9 C7
Alvington **457**	9 B6
Amberley	11 E6
Ampney Crucis **561**	11 H6
Ampney St Mary **119**	11 H6
Ampney St. Peter **107**	11 H6
Andoversford **547**	10 G4
Apperley	10 E3
Arlingham **377**	8 C5
Arlington	11 H5
Ashchurch **5,999**	10 F2
Ashleworth **476**	8 D3
Ashley **107**	11 F6
Ashton Keynes	11 G7
Aston Magna	10 J2
Aston Subedge **80**	10 H2
Aust **450**	9 B7
Avening **1,038**	11 F6
Awre **1,614**	8 C5
Aylburton **372**	9 B6
Badgeworth **1,168**	10 F4
Badminton **248**	11 E8
Bagendon **240**	11 G5
Barnsley **142**	11 H6
Barrington **201**	11 J5
Barton	10 H3
Batsford **142**	10 J2
Baughspring	9 B6
Baunton **266**	11 G6
Beachley	9 B7
Bentham	10 F4
Berkeley **1,550**	9 C6
Berry Hill	8 B5
Beverstone **134**	11 E7
Bevington	9 C6
Bibury **570**	11 H5
Birdlip	10 F5
Birdwood	8 D4
Bishop's Cleeve **7,186**	10 F3
Bisley-with-Lypiatt **2,118**	11 F5
Bitton **9,033**	9 C9
Blaisdon **253**	8 C4
Blakeney	8 C5
Bledington **424**	10 K4
Blockley **1,668**	10 J2
Boddington **260**	10 F3
Bournes Green	11 F6
Bourton-on-the-Hill **321**	10 J3
Bourton-on-the-Water **2,905**	10 J4
Box	11 E6
Boxbush	8 D5
Boxwell with Leighterton **210**	11 E7
Breadstone	9 C6
Bream **3,556**	8 B5
Bridgeygate	9 C9
Brierley	8 B4
Brimpsfield **266**	11 F5
Broad Campden	10 J2
Broadwell **351**	10 J3
Broadwell Lane End	8 B5
Brockhampton	10 G4

Brockweir	9 B6
Brockworth **6,649**	10 F4
Bromsberrow **182**	*
Brookethorpe-with-Whaddon **300**	11 E5
Buckland **247**	10 H2
Bulley	8 D4
Cainscross **5,879**	*
Calmsden	11 G5
Cam **8,099**	9 D6
Cambridge **1,792**	9 D6
Chaceley **120**	10 E3
Chalford **4,677**	11 F6
Charfield **2,231**	9 D7
Charingworth	10 J2
Charlton Abbots	10 G3
Charlton Kings **7,923**	10 F4
Chedworth **763**	11 H5
Cheltenham **86,996**	10 F4
Chepstow	9 B7
Cherington **119**	11 F6
Chipping Campden **1,997**	10 J2
Chipping Sodbury **4,596**	9 D8
Christchurch	8 B5
Churcham **630**	8 D4
Churchdown **10,319**	10 F4
Cinderford **7,653**	8 C5
Cirencester **17,085**	11 G6
Clapton-on-the-Hill **94**	10 J4
Clearwell	8 B5
Cleeve Hill **3,672**	10 G3
Clifford's Mesne	8 D4
Coaley **779**	9 D6
Coalpit Heath	9 C8
Coates **463**	11 G6
Coberley **284**	10 F4
Codrington	9 D8
Cold Ashton **239**	9 D9
Cold Aston **214**	10 H4
Coleford **5,069**	8 B5
Colesbourne **119**	11 G5
Coln Rogers	11 H5
Coln St. Aldwyn's **260**	11 J5
Coln St. Dennis **192**	11 H5
Compton Abdale **126**	10 H4
Condicote **137**	10 J3
Coombe Hill **3,145**	10 F3
Corse **534**	*
Cowley **311**	11 F5
Cranham **452**	11 F5
Cromhall **814**	9 C7
Cromhall Common	9 C7
Culkerton	11 F6
Cutsdean **72**	10 H3
Daglingworth **246**	11 G6
Daylesford	10 K3
Deerhurst **887**	10 E3
Didbrook	10 H3
Didmarton **429**	11 E7
Dixton	10 G3
Dodington **8,715**	9 D8
Donnington (Stow-on-the-Wold) **74**	10 J3
Donnington	8 C2
Doughton	11 E7
Dowdeswell **174**	10 G4
Down Ampney **502**	*
Down Hatherley **433**	10 E3
Doynton **303**	9 D9
Draycott	10 J2
Driffield **146**	11 H6
Drybrook **2,742**	8 C4
Dumbleton **510**	10 G2
Duntisbourne Abbots **227**	11 G5
Duntisbourne Leer	11 G5
Duntisbourne Rouse **81**	11 G5
Dursley **5,867**	9 D6
Dymock **1,283**	8 C3
Dyrham & Hinton **277**	9 D9
Eastcombe	11 F6

Easter Compton	9 B8
Eastington with Northleach **1,462**	11 H5
Eastington (Leonard Stanley) **1,469**	9 D6
Eastleach **299**	11 J5
Ebrington **441**	10 J2
Edge End	8 B5
Edgeworth **85**	11 F5
Elberton	9 B7
Elkstone **226**	11 F5
Ellwood	8 B5
Elmore **198**	8 D4
Elmore Back	8 D4
Elmstone Hardwicke **362**	10 F3
Elton	8 D5
Engine Common	9 C8
English Bicknor **414**	8 B4
Evenlode **153**	10 J3
Ewen	11 G6
Fairford **2,919**	11 J6
Falfield **471**	9 C7
Farleys End	8 D4
Farmcote	10 H3
Farmington **100**	10 H4
Fiddington	10 F3
Flaxley	8 C4
Ford	10 H3
Forthampton **169**	10 E3
Fossebridge **1.421**	11 H5
Frampton Cotterell **5,989**	9 C8
Frampton Mansell	11 F6
Frampton on Severn **1,383**	8 D5
Frenchay	9 B8
Fretherne with Saul **640**	8 D5
Frocester **190**	9 D6
Fyfield	11 J6
Glasshouse Hill	8 C4
Gloucester **94,256**	10 E3
Golden Valley	10 F4
Gorsley	8 C3
Gotherington **994**	10 F3
Great Badminton	9 D8
Great Rissington **315**	10 J4
Great Washbourne	10 G2
Great Witcombe **90**	10 F5
Gretton	10 G3
Guiting Power **331**	10 H3
Hailes	10 G3
Hallen	9 B8
Halmore	9 C6
Ham & Stone **704**	9 C6
Hamfallow **1,124**	*
Hampnett **53**	*
Hanham **5,776**	9 C9
Hardwick	10 F3
Hardwicke **3,237**	8 D5
Harescombe **278**	11 E5
Haresfield **349**	11 E5
Harnhill	11 H6
Hartpury **663**	8 D3
Hasfield **136**	10 E3
Hatherop **151**	11 J6
Hawkesbury **1,145**	9 D7
Hawkesbury Upton	9 D7
Hawling **110**	10 H4
Hazleton **158**	10 H4
Hempsted	10 E3
Hewelsfield **410**	9 B6
Hidcote Boyce	10 J2
Highleadon & Rudford **214**	8 D4
Highnam **2,130**	8 D4
Hill **91**	9 C7
Hillesley & Tresham **518**	9 D7
Hinton **1,147**	9 D9
Horsley **767**	11 E6
Horton **362**	9 D8
Hucclecote **788**	*
Huntley **1,082**	8 D4
Hyde	11 F6

6

Place	Pop.	Ref.
Icomb	97	10 J4
Ingst		9 B7
Innsworth	1,827	*
Iron Acton	1,322	9 C8
Itchington		9 C8
Kemble	762	11 G6
Kempley	288	8 C3
Kempsford	1,229	11 J6
Kent's Green		8 D4
Kilcot		8 C3
Kineton		10 H3
King's Stanley	2,618	11 E6
Kingscote	328	11 E6
Kingswood (Bristol)	48,117	9 C9
Kingswood (Wotton-u-Edge)	1,232	9.D7
Latteridge		9 C8
Laverton		10 H2
Lechlade	2,293	11 J6
Leckhampton	3,973	10 F4
Leigh	331	10 E3
Leighterton with Boxwell	210	11 E7
Leonard Stanley	1,501	9 D6
Little Badminton		11 E8
Little Barrington		11 J5
Little Rissington	893	10 J4
Littledean	1,258	8 C5
Littleton on Severn		9 B7
Long Newnton	179	11 F7
Longborough	507	10 J3
Longford	1,209	10 E3
Longhope	1,491	8 C4
Longney	183	8 D5
Lower Cam		9 D6
Lower Lemington		10 K2
Lower Slaughter	215	10 J4
Lower Swell		10 J3
Lydney	7,413	9 B6
Maisemore	487	10 E3
Mangotsfield	5,150	9 C9
Mangotsfield Rural	5,389	*
Marshfield	1,464	9 D9
Maugersbury	150	10 J3
Meysey Hampton	517	11 H5
Mickleton	1,551	10 J1
Milbury Heath		9 C7
Milkwall		8 B5
Minchampton	5,173	11 E6
Minsterworth	440	8 D4
Miserden	429	11 F5
Mitcheldean	2,632	8 C4
Moreton Valence	226	8 D5
Moreton-in-Marsh	2,802	10 J3
Morton		9 C7
Nailsworth	5,242	11 E6
Naunton	309	10 H4
Netherend		9 B6
Newent	5,373	8 D3
Newland	923	8 B5
Newnham	1,192	8 C5
Newport		9 C6
Nibley		9 C8
North Cerney	541	11 G5
North Nibley	803	9 D7
Northleach with Eastington	1,462	10 H4
Northway		10 F2
Northwick		9 B8
Northwood Green		8 D4
Norton	407	10 E3
Notgrove	105	10 H4
Nympsfield	326	11 E6
Oakle Street		8 D4
Oakridge		11 F6
Oddington	387	10 K3
Old Sodbury		9 D8
Oldbury on Severn	695	9 B7
Oldbury on the Hill		11 E7
Oldland	13,855	9 C9
Olverston	2,045	9 B7
Over		9 B8
Owlpen	36	*
Oxenhall	223	*
Oxenton	184	10 F3
Ozleworth	31	*
Painswick	3,013	11 E5
Parkend		8 B5
Patchway	11,017	9 B8
Pauntley	158	*
Paxford		10 J2
Pendock		8 D3
Pilning & Severn Beach	2,767	9 B8
Pitchcombe	248	11 E5
Poole Keynes	158	11 G7
Poolhill		8 D3
Poulton	354	11 H6
Prescott	90	*
Prestbury	7,403	10 G3
Preston	251	11 H6
Preston		8 C2
Pucklechurch	2,921	9 C9
Purton		9 C6
Quedgeley	7,352	11 E5
Quenington	514	11 J6
Randwick	1,470	11 E5
Rangeworthy	468	9 C8
Redbrook		8 B5
Redmarley D'Abitot	774	8 D3
Redwick		9 B8
Rendcombe	212	11 G5
Rockhampton	176	9 C7
Rodborough	5,367	*
Rodley		8 D5
Rodmarton	247	11 F6
Ruardean	1,435	8 B4
Ruardean Woodside		8 B4
Rudford & Highleadon	214	8 D4
Rudgeway		9 C8
Ruspidge	2,425	8 C5
Ryton		8 D3
St Briavels	1,329	9 B6
Saintbury	76	10 H2
Salperton		10 H4
Sandhurst	458	10 E3
Sapperton	370	11 F6
Saul		8 D5
Sevenhampton	376	10 G4
Severn Beach & Pilning	2,767	9 B8
Sezincote	93	10 J3
Sharpness		9 C6
Sheepscombe		11 E5
Sheperdine		9 B7
Sherborne	293	10 J4
Shipton	317	10 G4
Shipton Moyne	293	*
Shorncote		11 G6
Shurdington	2,242	10 F4
Shuthonger		10 F2
Siddington	1,345	11 G6
Siston	2,155	9 C9
Slad		11 E5
Slimbridge	1,113	9 D6
Snowshill	156	10 H2
Somerford Keynes	410	11 G7
Soundwell		9 C9
South Cerney	2,890	11 G6
Southam	760	10 G3
Southrop	223	11 J6
Standish	237	*
Stanton	222	10 H2
Stanway	322	10 H3
Staunton	542	8 D3
Staunton Coleford	267	*
Staverton	680	10 F4
Stinchcombe	410	9 D6
Stoke Gifford	12,342	9 C8
Stoke Orchard	312	10 F3
Stone & Ham	704	9 C7
Stonehouse	6,749	11 E6
Stow-on-the-Wold	1,999	10 J3
Stratton		11 G6
Stroat		9 B7
Stroud	11,677	11 E5
Sudeley	92	*
Sudgrove		11 F5
Swell	331	*
Swindon	1,780	10 F3
Syde	32	11 F5
Syreford		10 G4
Tarlton		11 F6
Taynton	403	8 D4
Teddington	420	10 F3
Temple Guiting	367	10 H3
Tetbury	4,618	11 F6
Tetbury Upton	447	11 F6
Tewkesbury	9,488	10 F2
The Camp		11 F5
The Quarry		9 D6
Thornbury	12,617	9 C7
Thrupp	1,768	11 E6
Tibberton	621	8 D4
Tidenham	4,943	9 B7
Tirley	385	10 E3
Tockington		9 B8
Toddington	418	10 G3
Todenham	221	10 K2
Tormarton	366	9 D8
Tortworth	129	9 C7
Tresham & Hillesley	518	9 D7
Trow Green		8 B5
Turkdean	104	10 H4
Twigworth	434	10 E3
Twyning	1,513	10 F2
Twyning Green		10 F2
Tytherington	560	9 C7
Uckington	313	10 F3
Uley	1,121	9 D6
Up Hatherley	2,963	10 F4
Upleadon	231	8 D3
Upper Framilode		8 D5
Upper Lydbrook	2,323	8 B4
Upper Slaughter	204	10 J4
Upper Soudley		8 C5
Upper Swell		10 J3
Upton Cheney		9 C9
Upton St. Leonards	1,674	10 E3
Walton Cardiff	58	10 F3
Wanswell		9 C6
Wapley		9 D8
West Dean	12,139	*
West Littleton		9 D9
Westbury-on-Severn	1,737	8 D4
Westcote	197	10 J4
Westerleigh	3,054	9 C8
Weston Subedge	389	10 H2
Westonbirt with Lasborough	165	*
Whaddon with Brookthorpe	300	11 E5
Whelford		11 J6
Whitecroft		8 C5
Whiteshill & Ruscombe	1,266	11 E5
Whiteway		11 F5
Whitfield		9 C7
Whitminster	495	8 D5
Whittington	126	10 G4
Wibdon		9 B6
Wick & Abson	1,940	9 D9
Wick Rissington	103	10 J4
Wickwar	1,552	9 D7
Willersey	778	10 H2
Winchcombe	4,835	10 G3
Windrush	109	11 J5
Winson	59	11 H5
Winstone	221	11 F5
Winterbourne	8,811	9 C8
Withington	486	10 G4
Woodchester	1,073	11 E6
Woodcroft		9 B7
Woodmancote	2,912	10 G3
Woodmancote		11 G5
Woolaston	1,299	9 B6
Wormington		10 G2
Wotton-under-Edge	5,635	9 D7
Yanworth	124	11 H5
Yate	19,777	9 D8
Yorkleys		8 C5

Population figures are based upon the 1991 census and relate to the local authority or parish as constituted at that date. Places with no population figure form part of a larger local authority area or parish. Boundaries of local authority areas are shown on pages 4-5. Population figures in bold type.

*Parish not shown on maps pages 8-11 due to limitation of scale.

8 ROAD MAP Scale 4 miles to 1 inch

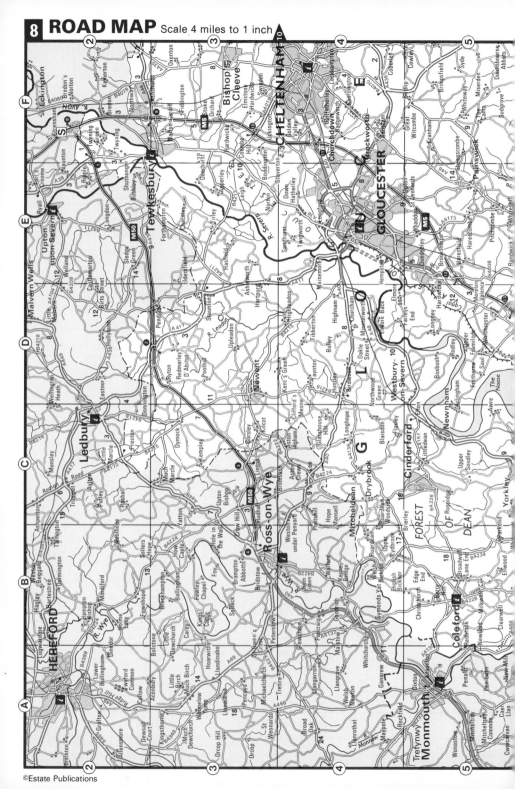

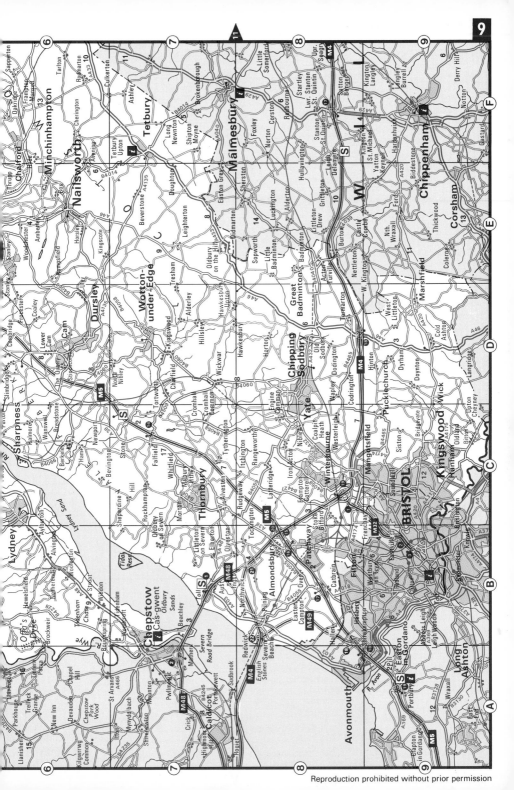

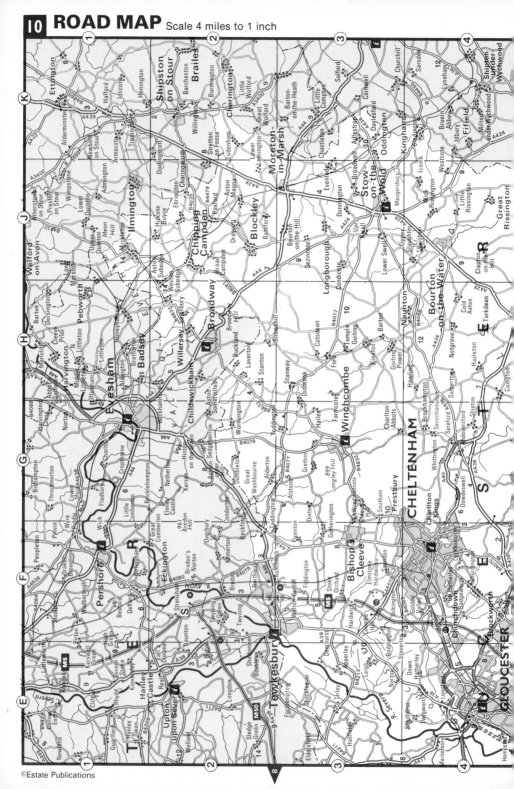

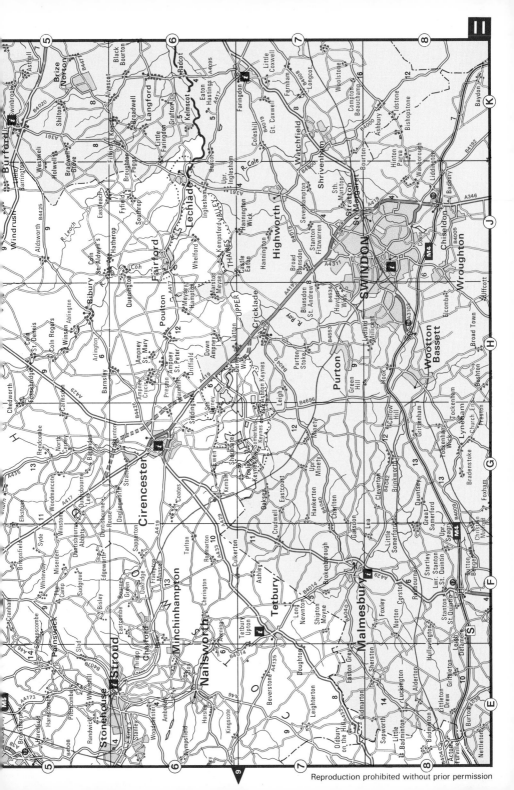

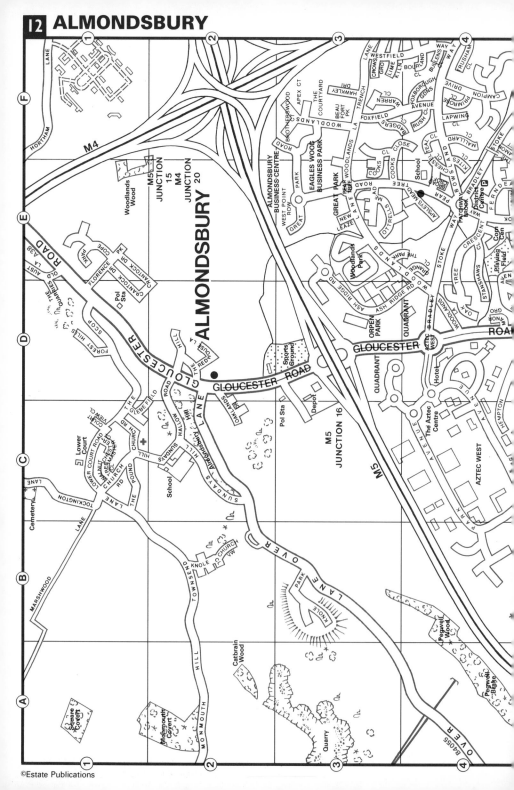

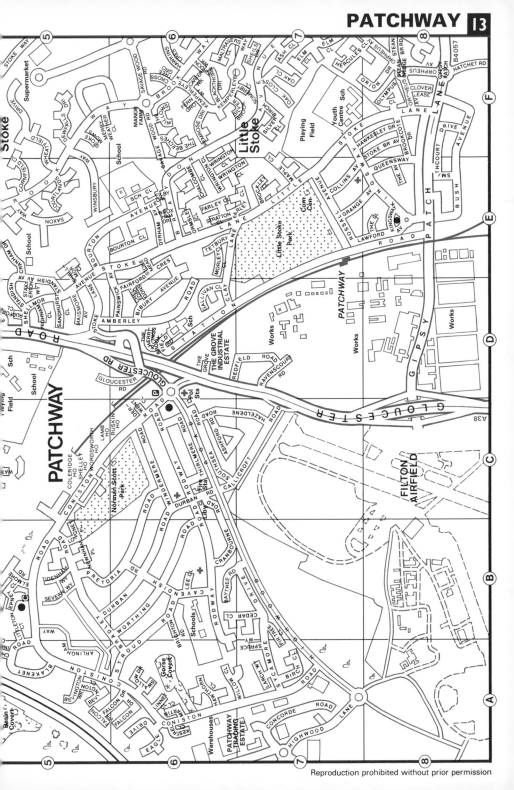

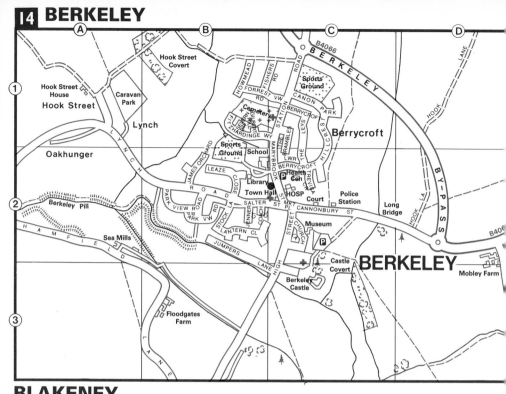

14 BERKELEY

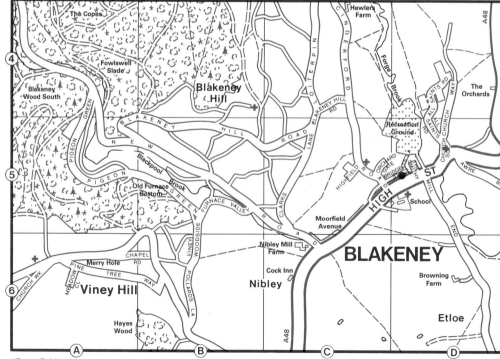

BLAKENEY

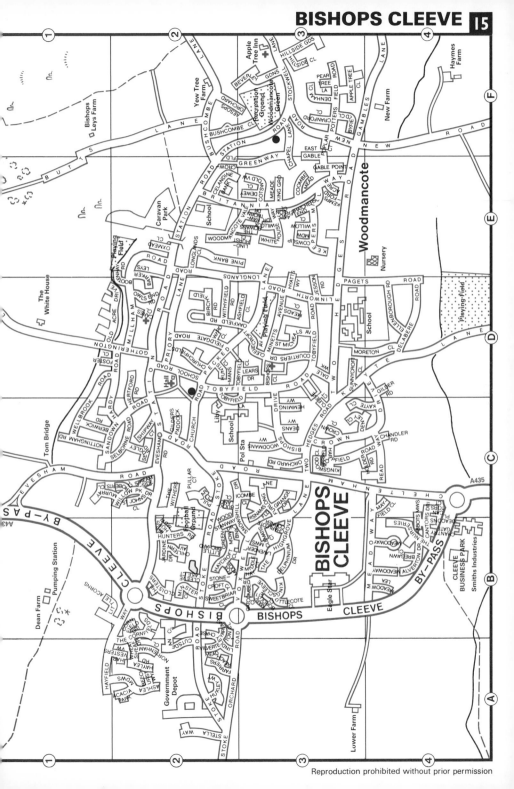

BISHOPS CLEEVE

Woodmancote

BOURTON-ON-
THE-WATER

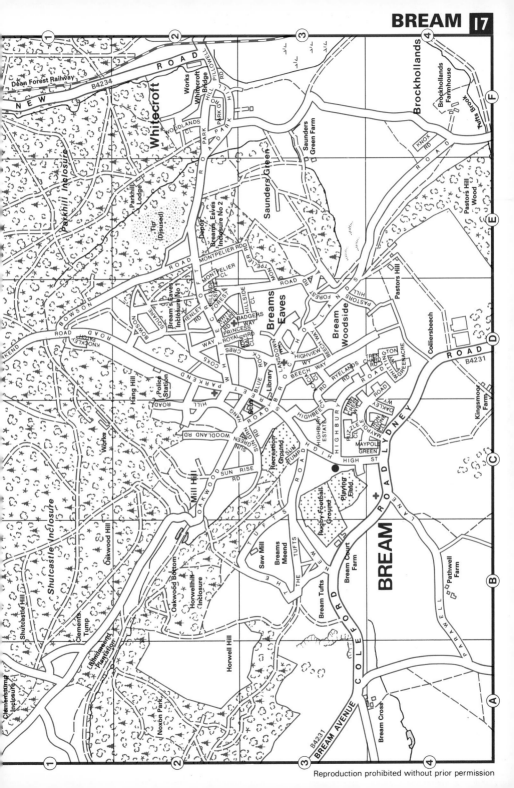

Ashmead Green

Upthorpe

Pear Orchard Farm

Upper Upthorpe Farm

Upthorpe Farm

HALMORE LANE

UPTHORPE

GREEN M CAM

STREET

PTON HILL

Dulkin Brook

Teetotal Valley

Upper Cam

Church Farm

ST GEORGES

CAM

ELM LODGE

School

Cam Mills

Millbank

Everlands

Noman Hill

Playing Field

Magistrates Court

DRAYCOTT BUSINESS PARK

River Cam

The Venning

Middle Mills

Courthouse Rd

Pol Sta

CHAPEL STREET

ORCHARD

FAIRMEAD

HIGH STREET

A4135

DRAYCOTT CRES

Everside Av

Jubilee

Morris Rd

Knapp

Masse

Drive

PITCH

Summerhayes

Woodview

Easide

The Croft

Nordown

Tilnor

The Orchard

Lansdown Rd

Tilsdown

Playing Field

Woodend Green Farm

Lower Cam

Lower Knapp Farm

Park Manor Lane

Tithe

Bowers

Pevel Lands

Withy

Bartholomews

Shuterman

Manor

Fairmead

Woodfield

MARMENT RD

Phillimore

Broadmere

Springfield

WOODFIELD

The Quarry

School

Crapen Road

Tindale

West End

ORCHARD

B4066

THE AVENUE

DURSLEY

FIELD LANE

ELSTUB LANE

Elstub Kennels

WOODEND

M5

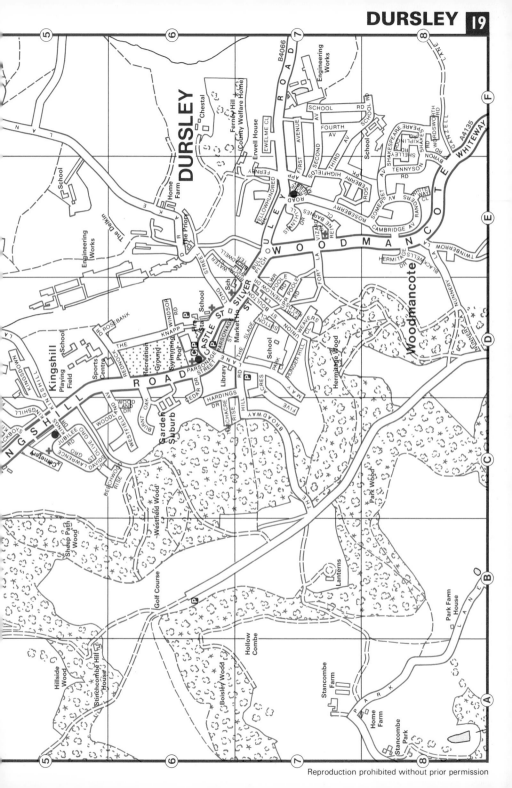

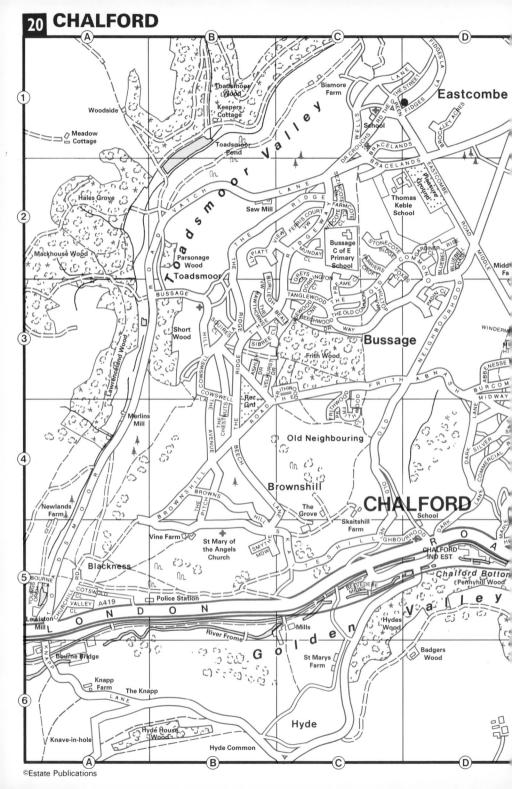

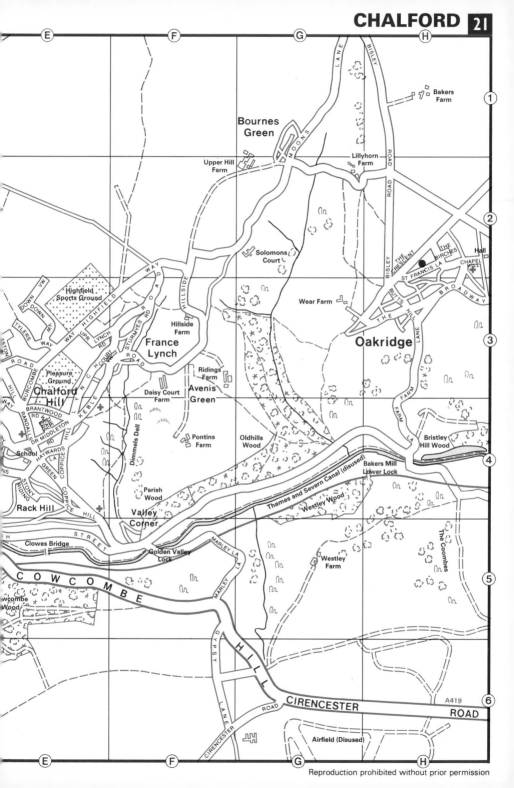

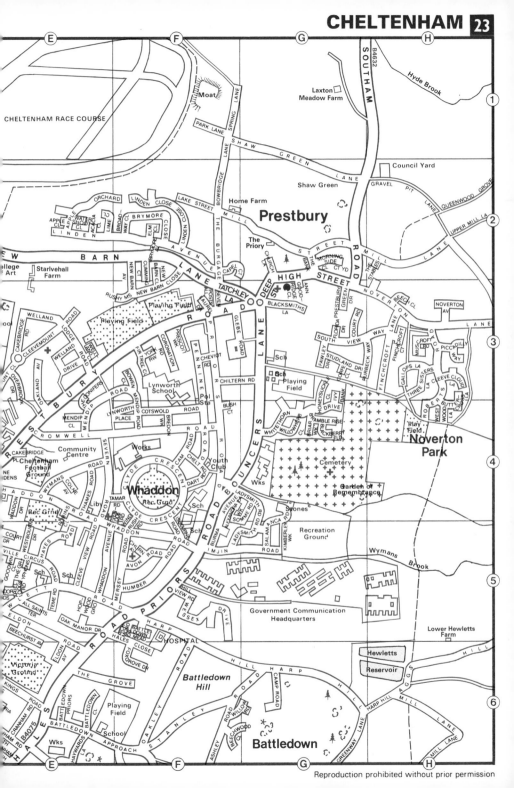

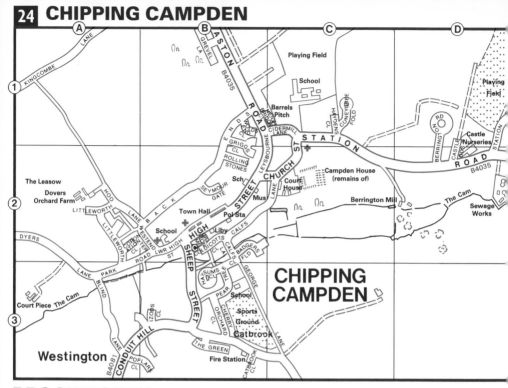

BROCKWORTH

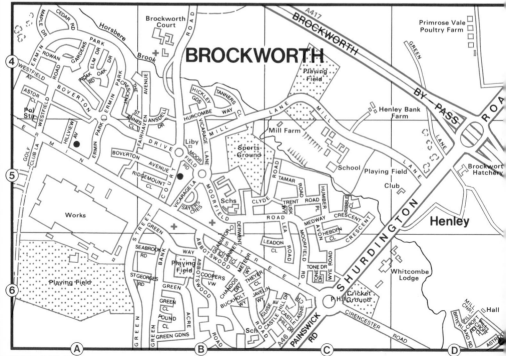

©Estate Publications

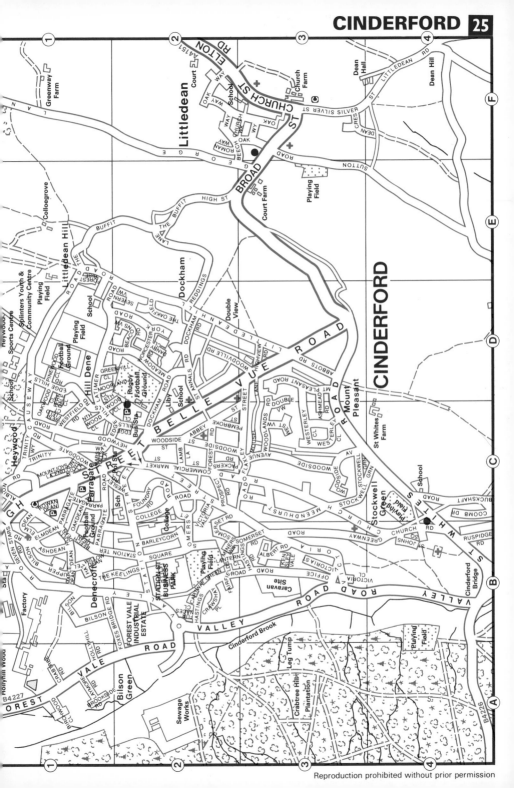

CINDERFORD

Littledean

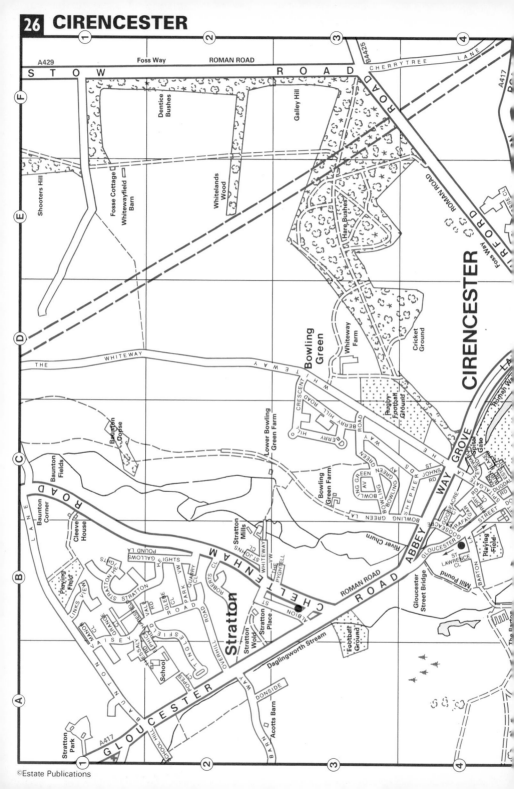

A429
Foss Way
ROMAN ROAD
S T O W R O A D

CHERRYTREE LANE
B4425
A417

Dentice Bushes

Galley Hill

Shooters Hill

Fosse Cottage

Whitewayfield Barn

Whitelands Wood

Hare Bushes

CIRENCESTER

ROMAN ROAD

Foss Way

Cricket Ground

Whiteway Farm

THE WHITEWAY

Bowling Green

Baunton Copse

Baunton Fields

Lower Bowling Green Farm

CRESCENT

BERRY HILL ROAD

THE WHITEWAY

Rugby Football Ground

Baunton Corner

Cleeve House

Bowling Green Farm

BOWLING GREEN LA

GREEN AV

ST JOHNS RD

SHEPHERDS

ABBEY WAY

GROVE LA

Goodacre

Gosacre

Spital Gate

St Lawrence CL

Playing Field

ROAD LANE

BAUNTON

Stratton Mills

ST JOHNS CL

WHITEWAY

PYGHELL

VW

River Churn

GLOUCESTER LA

BARTON

Mill Pound

Playing Field

LINKS VIEW

GALLOWS HEIGHTS

STRATTON

ROBERTS CL

CHELTENHAM ROAD

ALBION ST

Stratton Place

Gloucester Street Bridge

ST LAWRENCE RD

BAUNTON LANE

KANGLE

AISEY

GRANGE

TESSALY

PHIPPS

VAL RD

GLEBE CL

ROAD PARK

QUARRY

DINGLESPIE

OVERHILL ROAD

Stratton Wold

Stratton

School

ROMAN ROAD

ABBEY ROAD

Football Ground

Daglingworth Stream

Acotts Barn

DONSIDE

GLOUCESTER WAY

SCHOOL HILL

BARN

Stratton Park

A417

©Estate Publications

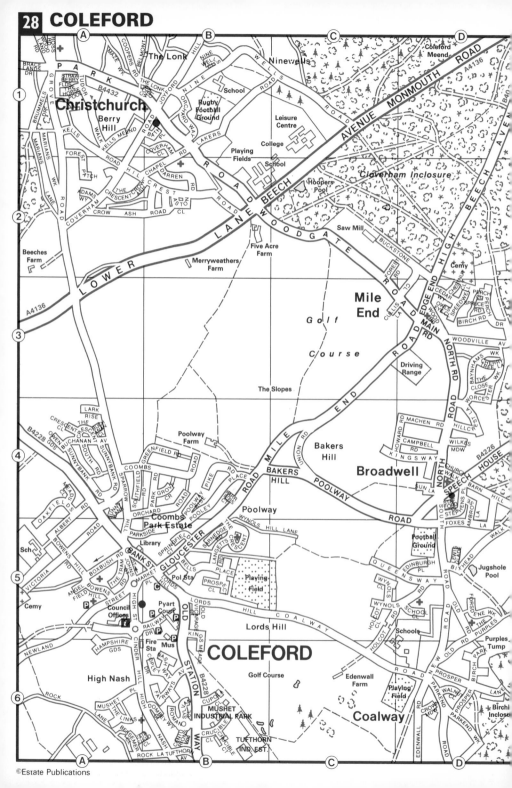

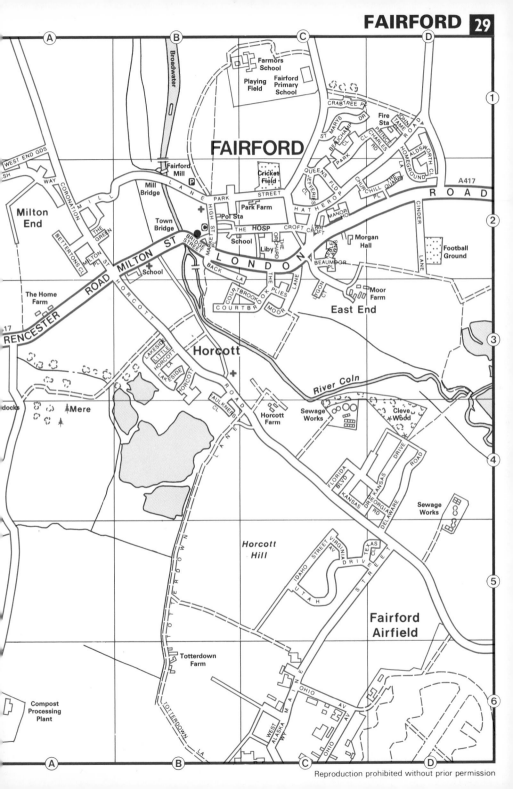

FAIRFORD

Milton End

The Home Farm

Horcott

Mere

East End

Morgan Hall

Football Ground

Moor Farm

River Coln

Cleve Wood

Horcott Farm

Sewage Works

Horcott Hill

Fairford Airfield

Sewage Works

Totterdown Farm

Compost Processing Plant

docks

Fairford Mill

Mill Bridge

Town Bridge

Cricket Field

Park Farm

Pol Sta

School

HOSP

Liby

Farmors School

Playing Field

Fairford Primary School

Fire Sta

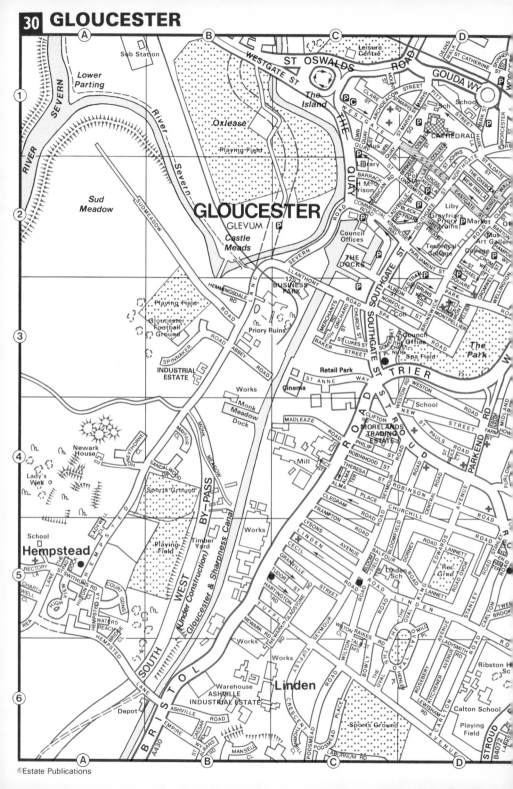

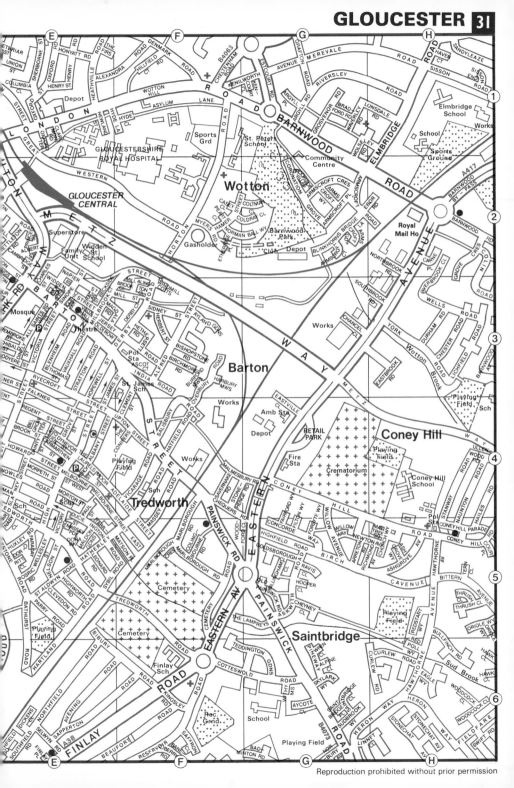

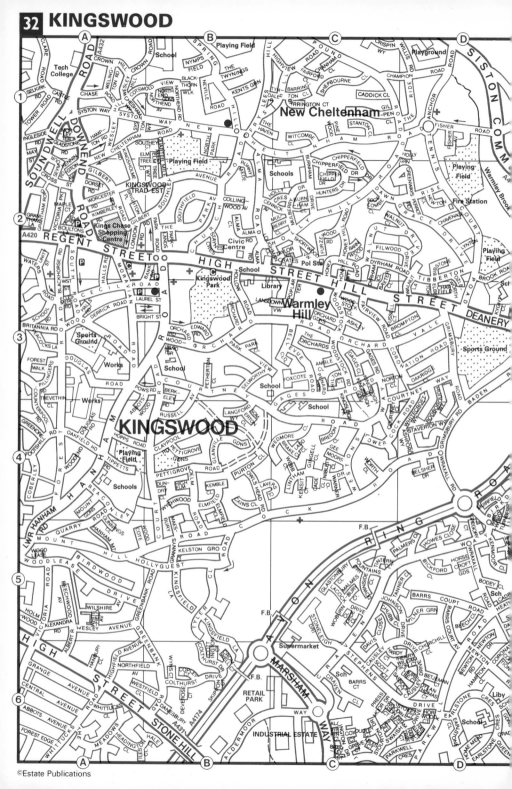

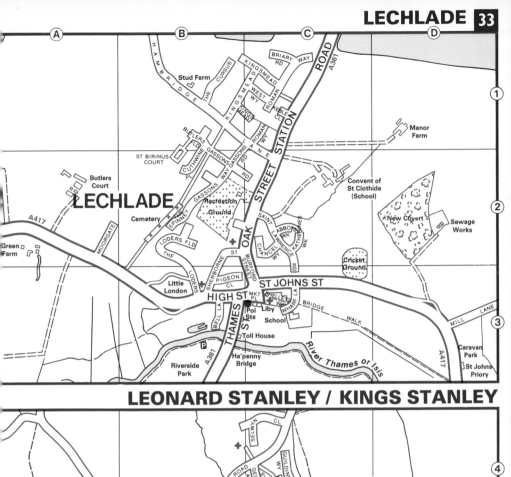

LECHLADE

Stud Farm, Butlers Court, St Birinus Court, Cemetery, Recreation Ground, Little London, Green Farm, Manor Farm, Convent of St Clothide (School), New Covert, Sewage Works, Cricket Ground, Riverside Park, Ha'penny Bridge, Toll House, Pol Sta, Liby, School, Caravan Park, St Johns Priory, River Thames or Isis

LEONARD STANLEY / KINGS STANLEY

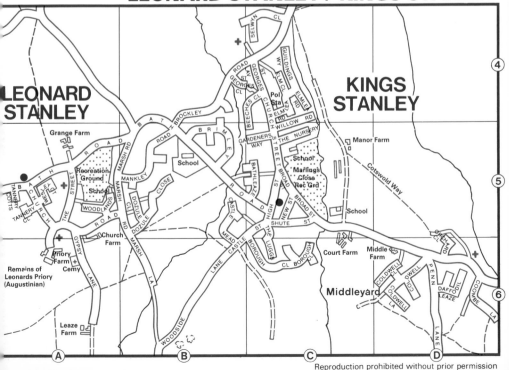

LEONARD STANLEY

KINGS STANLEY

Grange Farm, Recreation Ground, School, Tannery Cl, Woodlands, Church Farm, Priory Farm, Cemy, Remains of Leonards Priory (Augustinian), Leaze Farm, Manor Farm, School, Mallings Close Rec Grd, Pol Sta, The Nursery, Court Farm, Middle Farm, Middleyard, Cotswold Way

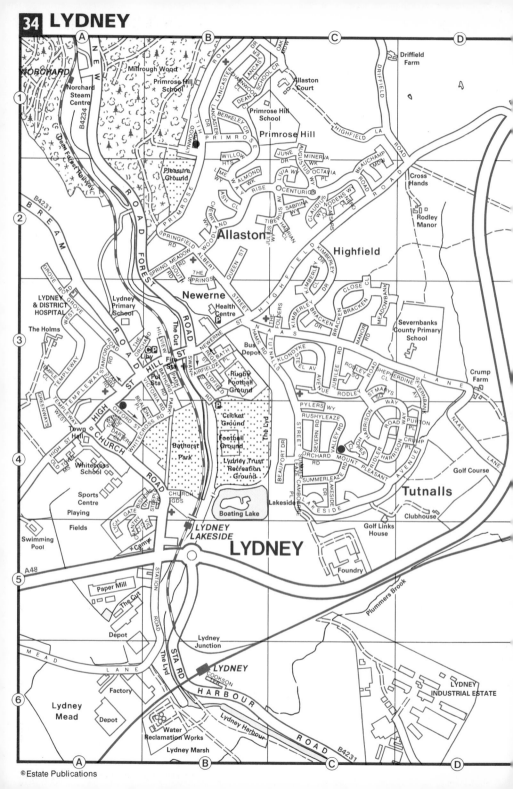

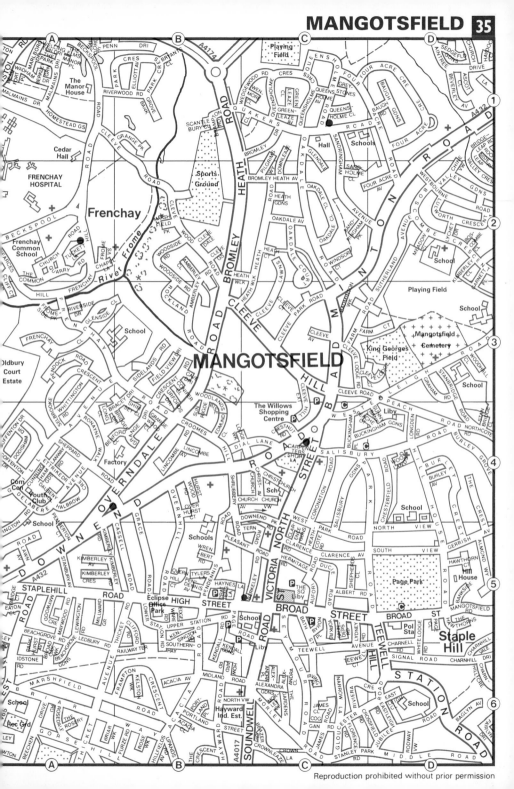

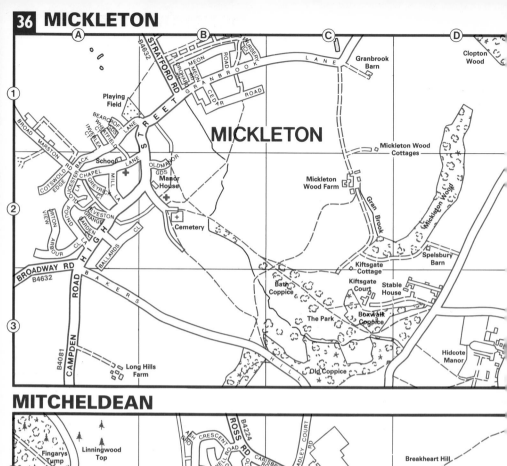

MICKLETON

Playing Field

STRATFORD RD B4632

MEON

PROPHETS

MEON ROAD

GRANBROOK

CEDAR ROAD

NURSERY ROAD

GRANBROOK LANE

Granbrook Barn

Clopton Wood

BROAD MARSTON RD

COTSWOLD EDGE

BEARCROFT

INKFIELD

WHEATFIELD

School

STREET

BACK LANE

CHAPEL LA

MILL LANE

GHETRICA

OLDMANOR

GDS

Manor House

Mickleton Wood Cottages

Mickleton Wood Farm

Mickleton Wood

GLOUCESTER

POUND CL

ORTON VIEW

ILVESTON

GRANGE

GARDEN

ARBOUR

HIGH

CL

Cemetery

BALLARDS

Gran Brook

BROADWAY RD B4632

ROAD

BAKERS

Kiftsgate Cottage

Bath Coppice

Kiftsgate Court

Stable House

Spelsbury Barn

Boxwalk Coppice

B4081

CAMPDEN ROAD

Long Hills Farm

The Park

Old Coppice

HILL

Hidcote Manor

MITCHELDEAN

Fingarys Tump

Linningwood Top

ASH

THE

CRESCENT

ROSS RD

B4224

CARISBROOK

OLD DEAN RD

DEANSWAY

BRADLEY CT

BRADLEY RD

Breakheart Hill

Harp Grove

HOLWELL ROAD

GLEBE CL

OAKHILL

MITCHELDEAN

Colla Meadow

Windman Hill

Community Centre

Recreation Ground

P

TOWNSEND

RANK XEROX BUSINESS PARK

Land Grove

Reservoir

Water Works

Warren Farm

Scully Grove

Tanners Grove

ORCHARD CL

CHURCHILL WY

WOODSIDE

HIGH ST

BROOK

Post Sta

Town Hall

WATTS ROW

THE BUILDING

P CP

AVENUE ROAD

PARKS

Wilderness Quarry

BARTON HILL

LADYGROVE BUSINESS PARK A4136

Mitcheldean Meend

THE STENDERS

STENDERS

Nature Reserve

NEW ST

BAYNHAM RD

COLCHESTER

WALWIN CL

EASTERN

MAY LANE

HANNER

ABENHALL

DEAN

GLOUCESTER RD

NEW ROAD

SILVER ST

A4136

School

Abenhall Lodge

Wilk Wo

Wilderness Farm

Judges Lodgings

Dene Magna School

Folly Farm

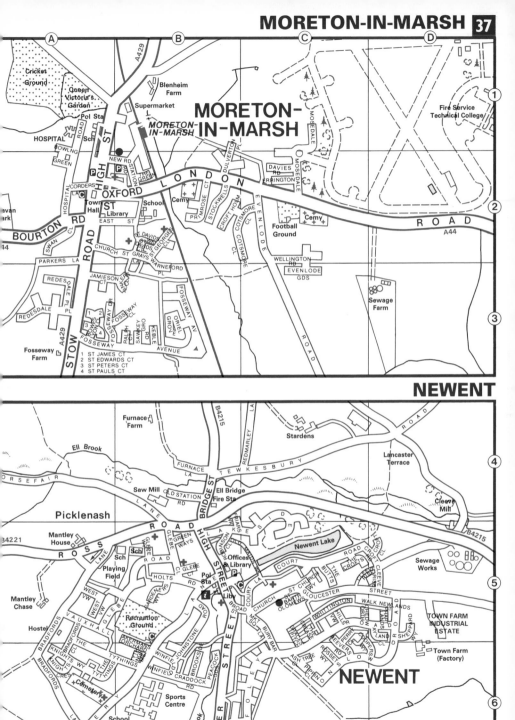

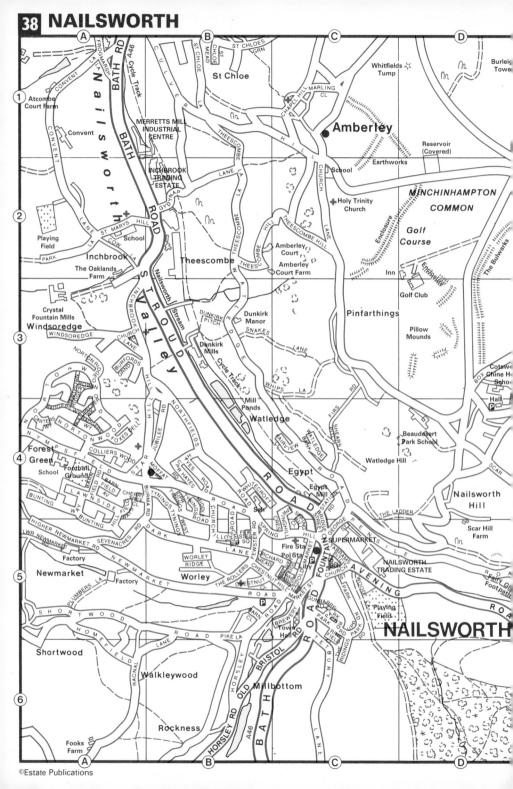

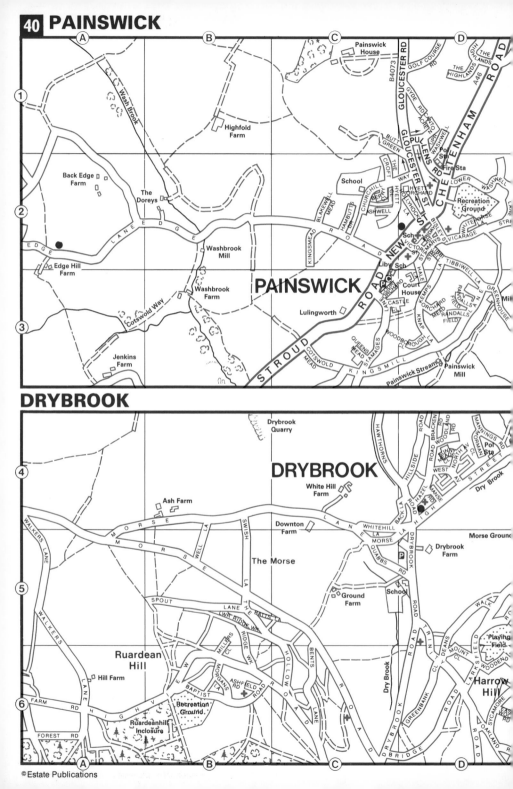

DRYBROOK

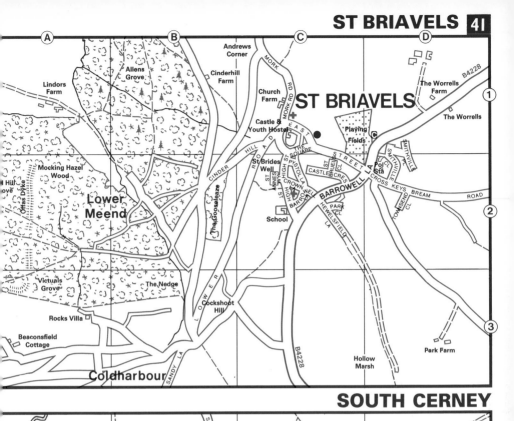

ST BRIAVELS

Andrews Corner, Allens Grove, Cinderhill Farm, Church Farm, The Worrells Farm, The Worrells, Lindors Farm, Castle & Youth Hostel, Playing Fields, MORK RD, EAST ROAD, HILL ROAD, CINDER ROAD, St Brides Well, St Annes St, Pistol La, High St, The Square, Crown La, CASTLE ST, BARR, CRES, STREET, BRUEN CL, CROSS KEYS, SMITHVILLE, SMITHVILLE CL, BREAM, ROAD, TOWNSEND CL, Pol Sta, BARROWELL, PARK CL, HEWELSFIELD LA, The Goosaleaze, Mocking Hazel Wood, Lower Meend, Offas Dyke, Hill ove, School, Victuals Grove, The Nedge, Cockshoot Hill, Rocks Villa, Beaconsfield Cottage, SANDY LA, LOWER ROAD, B4228, Park Farm, Hollow Marsh, Coldharbour

SOUTH CERNEY

Hill View Farm, Castle (site of), SILVER STREET, EDWARDS COLLEGE, Crane Farm, SOUTH CERNEY, Chapter Manor, BOW WOW, River Churn, TIMBRELLS CL, Hall, CHURCH LA, SCHOOL LA, CHURN WAY, CLARKS LA, MILL CL, BOXBUSH CL, BOX BUSH, THE CLOSE, ROBERT, FRANKLIN, LAKESIDE, ROAD, FIELD, WILDMOORWAY LA, ROAD, Upper–Up, RIVER WAY, BOW WOW, MEAD, LANGET, JUBILEE CL, GDS, HIGH STREET, BERKELEY, BERKELEY, BROADWAY, SUDELEY, HAM LANE, STATION ROAD, PADBROOK CL, PADBROOK, WILLOW GRO, HUXLEY, KINGFISHER PL, LENNARDS, WY, Recreation Ground, The Downs Farm, Works, School, THE LEAZE, THE CLOSE, BEAVER CL, OAK WAY, PENNY, STONE, LANE

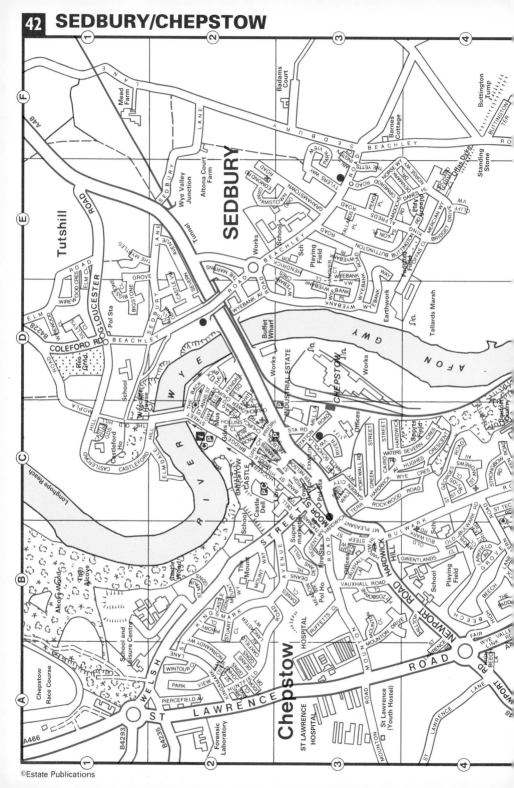

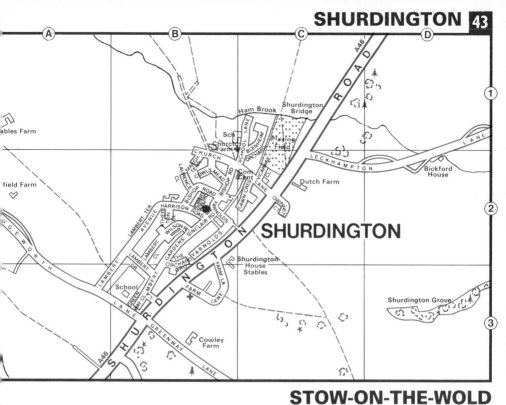

SHURDINGTON

STOW-ON-THE-WOLD

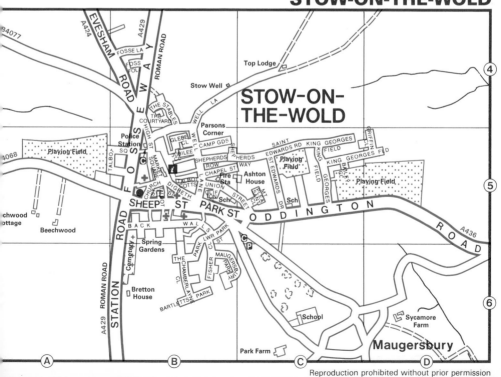

STOW-ON-THE-WOLD

Maugersbury

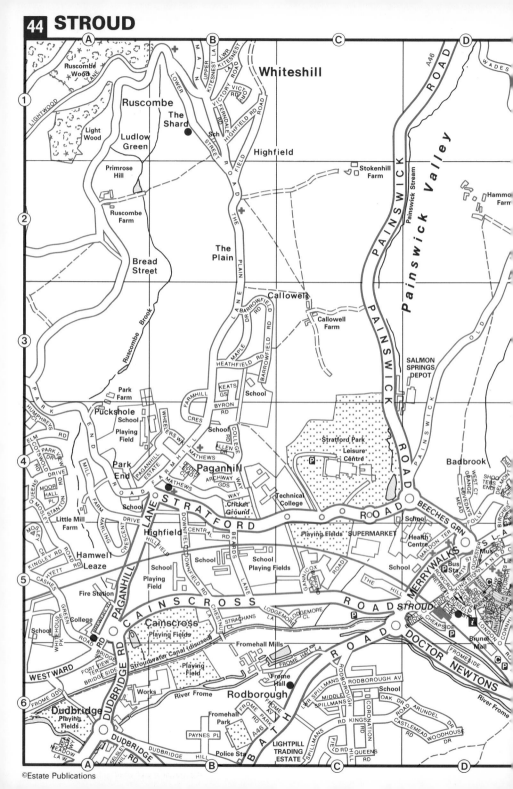

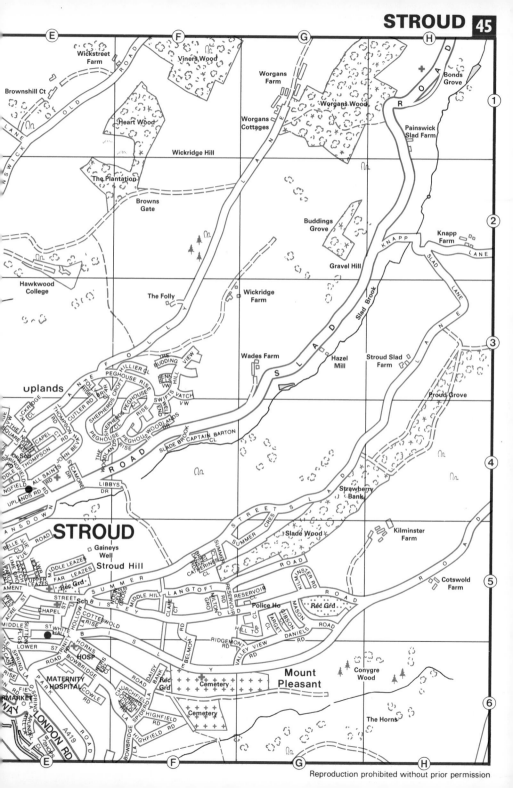

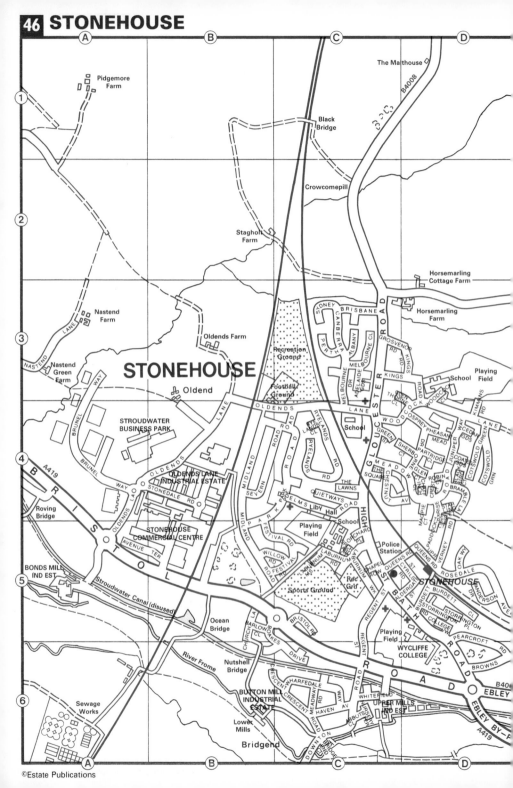

STONEHOUSE

Pidgemore Farm

The Malthouse

B4008

Black Bridge

Crowcomepill

Stagholt Farm

Horsemarling Cottage Farm

Horsemarling Farm

Nastend Farm

Oldends Farm

Recreation Ground

SIDNEY

BRISBANE

CANBERRA

PERTH

ALBANY

GROSVENOR

KINGS

Nastend Green Farm

Oldend

Football Ground

MELBOURNE

ADELAIDE

BOURNE CL

KINGS

MELB

THORNE

School

Playing Field

STROUDWATER BUSINESS PARK

OLDENDS

LANE

School

WOO

GREEN

OSPREY

PHEASANT

MEAD

COTSWOLD GREEN

BRUNEL WAY

SEVERN ROAD

RYELANDS

RYELANDS CL

RYELANDS RD

SHERBO

CT

PARTRIDGE

DR

JUNIPER

GDS

JUCOAT

COTSWOLD GRN

OLDENDS LANE INDUSTRIAL ESTATE

STONEDALE RD

THE LAWNS

QUIETWAYS

MEADOW

CHESTNUT

SQUARE

GLEN

ROBIN

CRISE

MAPLE

BRAMBLE LA

OAK WY

ROVING Bridge

OLDENDS LA

AVENUE TER

MIDLAND ROAD

PARK

ELMS

Liby Hall

School

HIGH

ROAD

LABURNUM

ORCHARD

Police Station

BURDETT

ANDERSON AVE

STONEHOUSE COMMERCIAL CENTRE

FESTIVAL RD

Playing Field

ST

CHAPEL

QUEENS RD

CYRIL

QUEENS RD

CIRL

ROSEDALE

BONDS MILL IND EST

WILLOW RD

FESTIVAL

Rec Grd

ALDERGATE

BURDETT RD

STORRINGTON PL

STONEHOUSE

Stroudwater Canal (disused)

Sports Ground

REGENT ST

BATH

COLLEGE RD

PEARCROFT RD

BROWNS RD

Ocean Bridge

BARLOW

BOOKES

CHURCH LA

BRISTOL RD

DRIVE

Playing Field

WYCLIFFE COLLEGE

EBLEY

B40

River Frome

Nutshell Bridge

WHARFEDALE

CRESCENT

MEADWAY ROAD

HAVEN AV

WHITEFIELD

ROAD

B4

EBLEY BY-P

A419

Sewage Works

BUTTON MILL INDUSTRIAL ESTATE

Lower Mills

UPPER MILLS IND EST

DOWNTON

ABBOTTS

Bridgend

A419

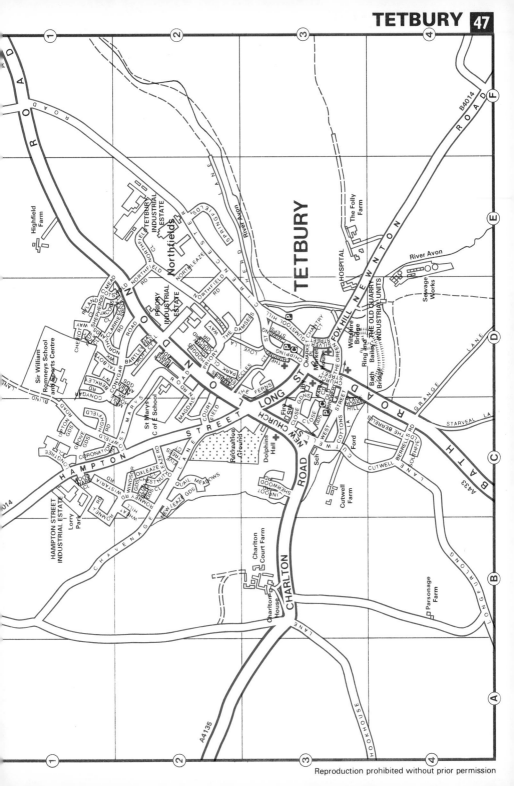

TETBURY

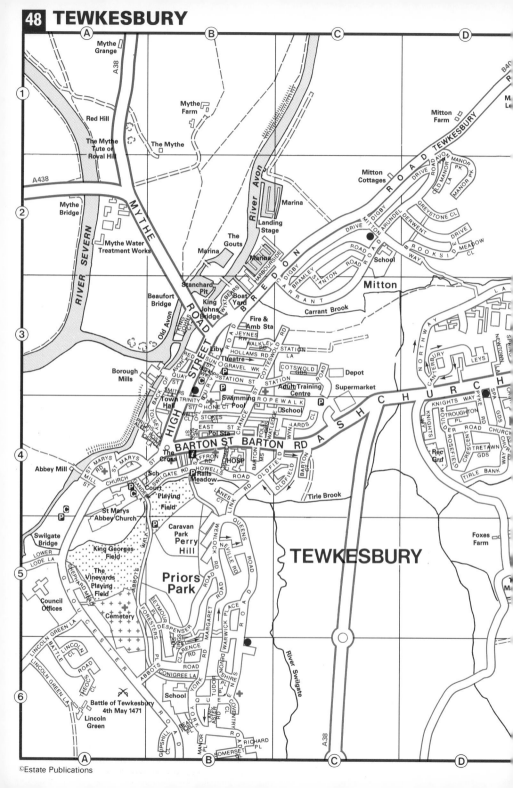

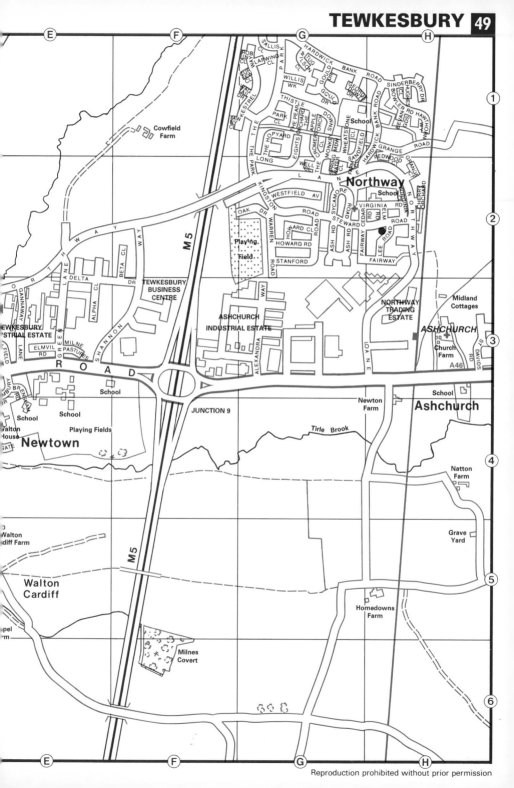

E F G H

1

Cowfield
Farm

WILLIS
WK

HARDWICK
BANK ROAD

SINDERBERRY DR

ROB
ING
CL
SLAPWING
CL

SALLIS
CL

PARK
HUG
GOULD

WILSON
DRY

BERRY
CL

HAWTHORN

HOBBY
KESTREL

THISTLE
DRY

THE PEARL

APPLE

GGUL
DR

BENHAM RD
HUGHES RD
GDS

M5

School

HIGHFIELD

THE MONKS
PORCH

WHEATSTONE
CL

GRANGE
ROAD
GRANGE

REDWOOD

HARDWICK BANK ROAD

CL

THE
HO

CROMER
CL

SAVOFIELD

Northway

PYARD

WELL

THE
LONG
THE
PARK

EIGHTS

SPRING
MDW

School

HENRY CL
ORCHARD

2

Westfield AV

SYCAMORE

Virginia

NORTHWAY

THE
PARK
Playing.
Field.

KINGSTON

OAK
DR

WARREN

HOWARD ROAD

STEWARD

STEWARD
CEDAR
RD

ELM
RD

VIRGINIA

FAIRWAY

OAK

HOWARD RD

ASH HD

AVON

LEE ROAD

ROAD

ROAD
STANFORD

ASH RD

FAIRWAY

TEWKESBURY
BUSINESS
CENTRE

DELTA

BETA CL

ALPHA

ASHCHURCH
INDUSTRIAL ESTATE

ALEXANDRA

WAY

NORTHWAY
TRADING
ESTATE

Midland
Cottages

ASHCHURCH

3

EWKESBURY
'STRIAL ESTATE

GANNAWAY
LANE

MILNE
PASTURES

ELMVIL
RD

SHANNON

GREEN
LANE

R O A D

LANE

Church
Farm

ST DAVIDS

A46

JUNCTION 9

School

School
School

Newton
Farm

Natton
Farm

School

Ashchurch

4

Walton
House
GATE

Playing Fields

Newtown

Tirle Brook

Walton
diff Farm

M5

Grave
Yard

5

Walton
Cardiff

pel
m

Homedowns
Farm

6

Milnes
Covert

E F G H

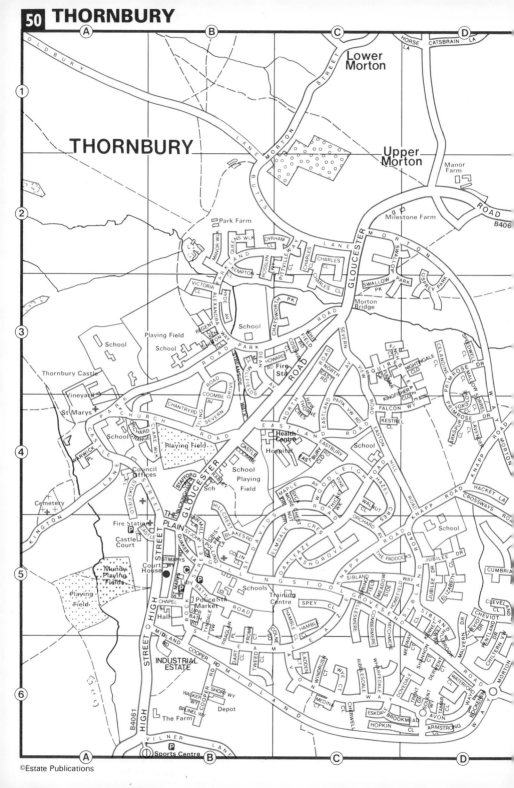

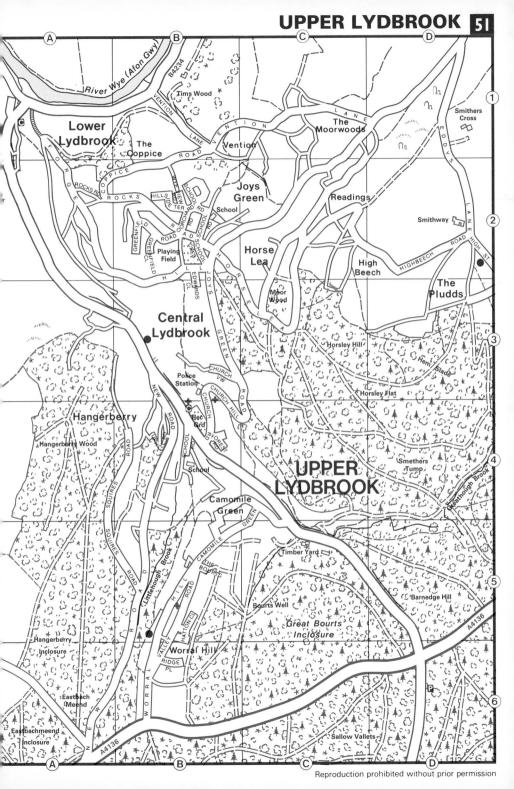

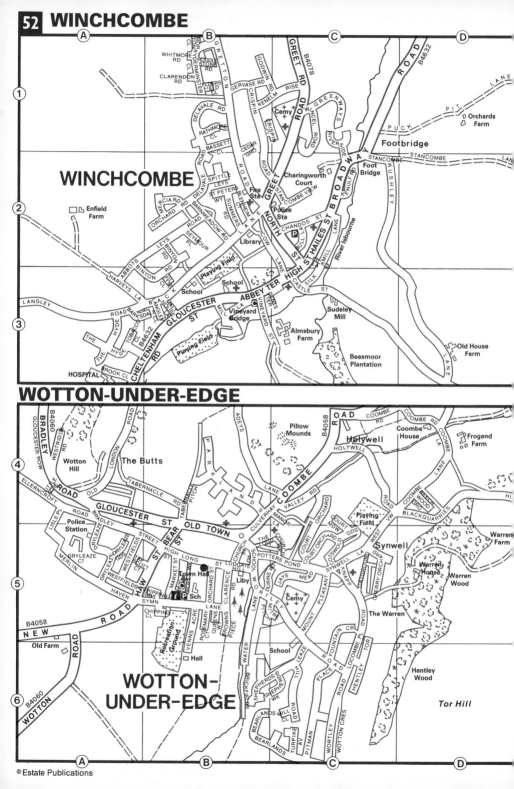

52 WINCHCOMBE

WINCHCOMBE

WOTTON-UNDER-EDGE

WOTTON–UNDER-EDGE

© Estate Publications

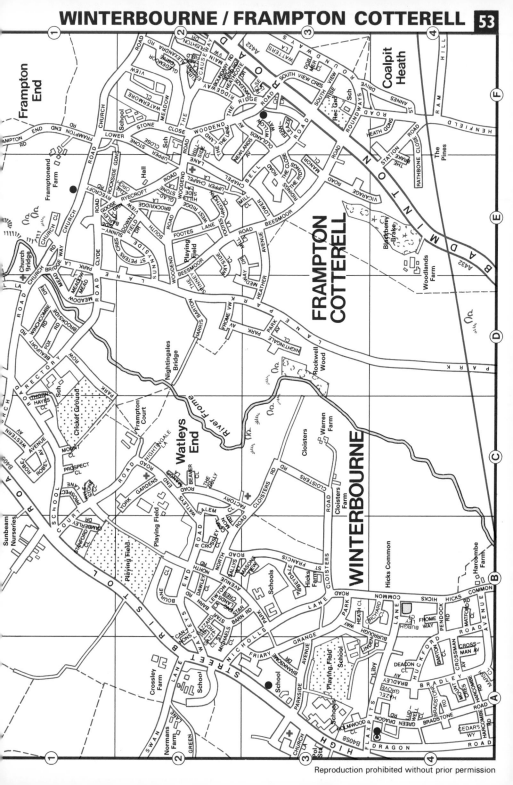

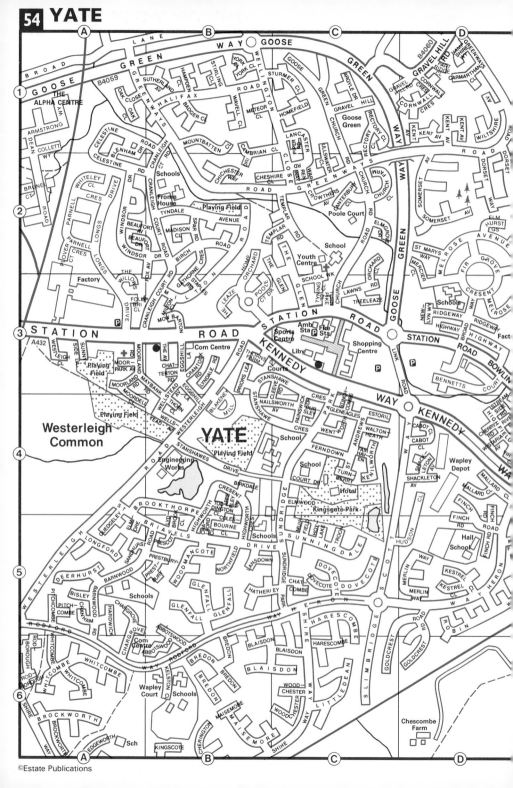

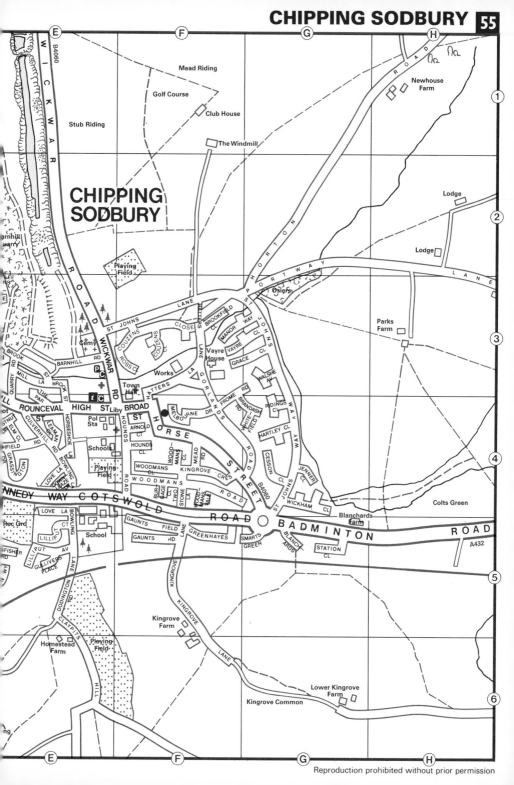

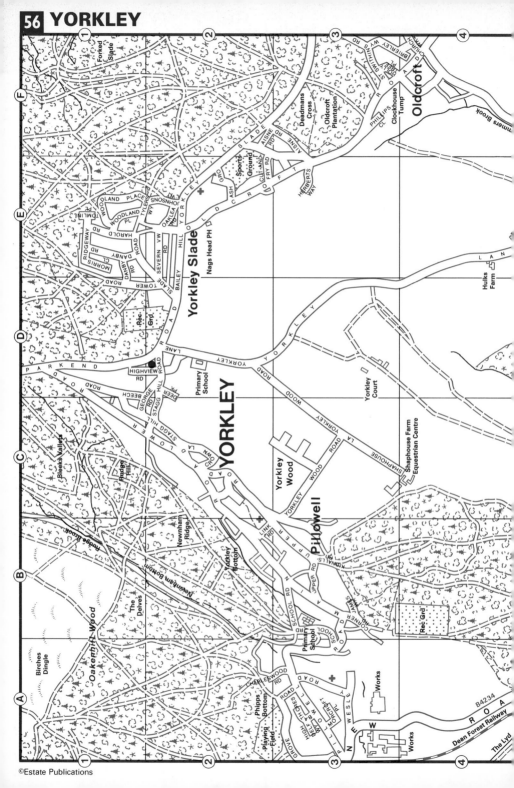

The Index includes some names for which there is insufficient space on the maps. These names are preceded by an * and are followed by the nearest adjoining thoroughfare.

ALMONDSBURY/ PATCHWAY

Amberley Rd	13 D6
Apsleys Mead	12 E4
Arlingham Way	13 A5
Ash Clo	13 F7
Ash Ridge Rd	12 D4
Ashford Rd	13 C6
Atwell Dri	12 D4
Badgers Clo	12 F3
Bevington Clo	13 A5
Bevington Wk	13 A5
Bibury Av	13 D6
Birch Clo	13 A7
Blakeney Rd	13 A5
Bourland Clo	12 F4
Bourton Av	13 E5
Bourton Clo	13 E6
Bowsland Way	12 E4
Brackendean	12 E4
Bradley Rd	13 A6
Bradley Stoke Way	12 D4
Brighton Rd	13 B6
Broad Croft	12 E4
Brockley Clo	13 E7
Brook Way	12 E4
Brookcote Dri	13 F8
Brookfield Rd	13 D6
Bullens Clo	12 F4
Bush Av	13 E8
Callicroft Rd	13 C6
Carter Wk	13 F6
Cavendish Rd	13 B6
Cedar Clo	13 B7
Chalcombe Clo	13 E6
Chelford Gdns	13 D6
Chessel Clo	13 D6
Chestermaster Clo	12 C1
Chillington Ct	13 A5
Church Rd	12 C1
Clay La	13 D6
Collins Av	13 E7
Concorde Rd	13 A7
Coniston Rd	13 A6
Cooks Clo	12 E3
Cope Park	12 E1
Cornfield Clo	13 E5
Court Vw Clo	12 C1
Cranbourne Rd	13 B6
Cranham Dri	13 E5
Crantock Dri	12 D1
Cross Tree Gro	13 F6
Crows Grove	12 F3
Derwent Clo	13 C6
Dewfalls Dri	13 F5
Durban Rd	13 C6
Dyrham Av	13 E6
Eagle Dri	13 A6
Elm Clo	13 F7
Elmore Rd	13 B5
Elms Gro	13 D5
Epney Clo	13 B5
Fairford Cres	13 D6
Falcon Dri	13 A6
Farley Clo	13 E6
Fern Gro	13 F6
Ferndean	12 E4
Filby Dri	13 E6
Firtree Clo	13 B7
Florence Park	12 D1
Forest Hills	12 D1
Foxborough Gdns	12 F4
Foxfield Av	12 F3
Gipsy Patch La	13 D8
Gloucester Rd	13 C8
Grange Av	12 E4
Grange Clo	12 E4
Great Park Rd	13 F8
Hallow Dri	12 C2
Hatchet Rd	13 F8
Hawkins Cres	13 F6
Hawkley Dri	12 F3
Hawkesley Dri	13 F8
Hawthorn Clo	13 A6
Hazeldene Rd	13 C7
Hempton La	12 C4
Hercules Clo	13 F7
Highnam Clo	13 D5
Highwood La	13 A7
Highwood Rd	13 A7
Hortham La	12 F1

INDUSTRIAL ESTATES:

Almondsbury Business Centre	12 F2
Eagles Wood Business Park	12 E3
Orpen Park Business Park	12 D3
Patchway Trading Estate	13 A6
Quadrant Business Centre	12 D3
The Grove Ind Est	13 D6
Jordon Wk	13 F6
Kestrel Clo	13 A6
Kingsway	13 E8
Kites Clo	12 E4
Knole Clo	12 B2
Knole Park	12 B3
Larch Way	13 A7
Lawford Av	13 E8
Lee Clo	13 B6
Lime Kiln	12 F3
Linnet Clo	13 A6
Little Stoke La	13 E7
Littleton Ct	13 B5
Longney Pl	13 B5
Lower Court Rd	12 C1
Maisemore Av	13 D5
Maltravers Clo	13 F6
Manor Gro	12 D4
Maple Clo	13 E7
Marshwood La	12 B1
Martin Clo	13 A6
Merryweather Clo	13 F6
Monmouth Hill	12 A2
Morley Clo	13 E6
New Leaze	12 E3
Newnham Pl	13 B5
Oak Clo	13 F7
Oak Tree Cres	13 F8
Oaklands Dri	12 C2
Old Aust La	12 E1
Olympus Clo	13 F8
Orion Dri	13 F8
Ormsley Clo	13 E6
Orpheus Av	13 F8
Ottrells Mead	12 E3
Over La	12 A4
Painswick Av	13 D6
Park Av	12 C4
Pear Tree La	12 E4
Pemrose Dri	13 F6
Pretoria Rd	13 B5
Primrose Clo	12 F4
Queensway	13 E8
Ravenscourt Rd	13 D7
Redfield Rd	13 D7
Redhouse La	12 D2
Rodway Rd	13 B6
Rossall Av	13 E7
Rudford Clo	13 D5
Rush Clo	12 F4
Sandhurst Clo	13 D5
Savage Wood Rd	13 F6
School Clo	13 E6
Severn Way	13 B5
Shellmor Av	13 D5
Shellmor Clo	13 E5
Silverbirch Clo	13 F7
Silver Brook	13 F7
Smithcourt Dri	13 E8
Somerby Clo	13 F7
Southsea Rd	13 C6
Spruce Way	13 A7
Standish Av	13 D6
Stanshaws Clo	12 E4
Station Rd	13 D6
Staverton Way	13 D5
Stean Bridge Rd	13 F8
Stoke Br Av	13 F8
Stoke La	13 D5
Stoke Mead	13 E6
Stratton Clo	13 E6
Stroud Rd	13 A6
Sundays Hill	12 C2
Swallow Dri	13 A6
Sycamore Dri	13 A7
Tetbury Clo	13 E6
The Avenue, Bradley Stoke	12 D4
The Avenue, Patchway	13 E8
The Beeches	13 F6
The Close, Bradley Stoke	12 E4
The Close, Patchway	13 E8
The Common	13 D5
The Grove	13 D6
The Hill	12 D2
The Park	12 E3
The Pound	12 C1
The Quarries	12 D1
The Scop	12 C1
The Sherrings	13 D6
The Willows	13 F6
Thirlmere Rd	13 C6
Tidenham Way	13 B5
Tockington La	12 C1
Townsend La	12 B2
Walnut Tree Clo	12 C1
Warren Clo	12 F3
Waterside Dri	13 C5
Westfield Way	12 F3
Wheatfield Dri	13 F5
Willow Clo	13 A7
Windermere Rd	13 C6
Woodlands	12 F3
Woodlands La	12 D4
Worthing Rd	13 B6
Wrington Clo	13 E6
Wroxham Dri	13 E6

BERKELEY

Berkeley By-Pass	14 C1
Berrycroft	14 C1
Cannonbury St	14 C2
Canon Park	14 C1
Church La	14 C2
Coach Clo.	14 B2
Fishers Rd	14 B1
Fitzhardinge Way	14 B1
Forrest View Rd	14 B1
Gilbert Hill	14 B1
Hamfield La	14 A2
High St	14 C2
Hillcrest	14 C2
Hook La	14 D2
Howmead	14 B1
James Orchard	14 B2
Jenner Ct	14 B2
Jumpers La	14 B2
Lantern Clo	14 B2
Leaze Clo	14 B2
Lower Berrycroft	14 C2
Lynch Rd	14 A1
Marybrook St	14 C2
Park View Rd	14 B2
Salter St	14 B2
Severn Dri	14 B1
Station Rd	14 C1
Stock La	14 B2
The Brambles	14 C1
The Leys	14 C2
Trevisa Cres	14 C2

BISHOPS CLEEVE

Abbots Mws	15 B4
Acacia Pk	15 A2
Aesops Orchard	15 F2
Alverton Dri	15 B4
Anderson Clo	15 E3
Apple Tree Clo	15 F3
Ashfield Clo	15 D3
Ashlea Mdws	15 A2
Barker Leys	15 D2
Beechhurst Way	15 A2
Berwick Rd	15 C1
Beverley Gdns	15 F3
Bishfield Rd	15 D2
Bishops Cleeve By-Pass	15 B2
Bishops Clo	15 D3
Bishops Dri	15 C3
Bishops Mdws	15 B2
Bootenhay Rd	15 D2
Bregawn Clo	15 B4
Britannia Way	15 B4
Buckland Clo	15 C2
Bushcombe Clo	15 F2
Bushcombe La	15 F2
Butts La	15 E1
Byfield Clo	15 F3
Cantors Ct	15 C4
Cantors Dri	15 B4
Cares Clo	15 D2
Celandine Bank	15 E2
Chandler Rd	15 C4
Chantry Gate	15 B4
Chapel La	15 F3
Charlotte Corner	15 B3
Cheltenham Rd	15 C4
Chiltern Av	15 B2
Church Rd	15 C2
Churchfields	15 D2
Cleeve Ct	15 C3
Cleeve Lake Ct	15 B2
Cleevecroft Av	15 D3
Clematis Ct	15 B3
Coombe Meade	15 E3
Cornfield Dri	15 B2
Cotswold Vw	15 E3
Courtiers Dri	15 D3
Cowslip Meadow	15 E3
Cranford Clo	15 F3
Crowfield	15 E2
Crown Clo	15 C3
Crown Dri	15 C3
Cutsdean Clo	15 A2
Dale Walk	15 D3
Deacons Pl	15 B4
Deans Way	15 C3
Delabere Rd	15 D4
Delphinium Dri	15 B3
Denham Clo	15 F3
Denley Clo	15 C3
Dewey Clo	15 E3
East Gable	15 F3
Ellenborough Rd	15 D4
Evesham Rd	15 C1
Farriers Reach	15 A2
Fieldgate Rd	15 D2
Foster Clo	15 D1
Fox Moor	15 B2
Furlong La	15 C3
Gable Point	15 E3
Gambles La	15 F3
Gatcombe Clo	15 B3
Gilder Rd	15 D4
Gilders Paddock	15 C2
Gotherington La	15 D3
Grange Dri	15 C3
Green Meadow Bank	15 B2
Greenway	15 E3
Hardy Rd	15 C2
Harpfield Clo	15 C3
Harpfield Rd	15 B2
Harvesters Vw	15 A2
Hawthorn Dri	15 E3
Haycroft Clo	15 B2
Hayfield Way	15 A1
Haylea Rd	15 A2
Hemming Way	15 C3
Hertford Rd	15 D3
Hillside Clo	15 F3
Hillside Gdns	15 F3
Hisnams Field	15 C3
Holder Rd	15 C4
Hunters Rd	15 B2
Huntsmans Clo	15 D2
Huxley Way	15 A2
Hyatts Way	15 D3
Icombe Clo	15 C3
Jardine Dri	15 B2
Jesson Rd	15 D3
Kayte Clo	15 C4
Kayte La	15 D3
Keepers Mill	15 E3
Kempsford Acre	15 E3
Kingscleeve Dri	15 B3
Kingswood Clo	15 C3
Lavender Ms	15 B3
Lears Dri	15 D3
Lindhurst Clo	15 E3
Lindley Chase	15 A2
Linworth Rd	15 D3
Little Acorns	15 B1
Littlecote	15 B3
Little Orchard	15 B2
Longlands Clo	15 E2
Longlands La	15 D3
Marlborough Clo	15 B3
Mayfield Clo	15 C4
Meade King Gro	15 E3
Meadow Lea	15 B4
Meadoway	15 B4
Meads Clo	15 D3
Middle Hay Ct	15 B3
Millham Rd	15 D2
Minetts Av	15 D3
Minster Clo	15 B2
Moreton Clo	15 D4
Murray Clo	15 C2
New Rd	15 F3
Nortenham Clo	15 A2
Nottingham Rd*	15 C1
Oakfield Rd	15 D3
Old Acre Dri	15 D2
Orchard Rd	15 C3
Owls End Rd	15 D2
Oxmead Clo	15 E2
Pagets Rd	15 D3
Pear Tree La	15 F3
Pecked La	15 D2
Pine Bank	15 E2
Poplar Ct	15 F3
Potters Field Rd	15 F3
Priory La	15 D2
Pullar Clo	15 C2
Pullar Ct	15 C2
Read Way	15 C4
Roberts Clo	15 C2
St Johns Clo	15 C2
St Michaels Av	15 D3
Sandown Rd	15 B2
School Rd	15 D2
Sedgley Rd	15 C2
Selbourne Rd	15 C2
Shipway Ct	15 C2
Snowshill Dri	15 B3
Station Rd	15 A2
Stella Way	15 A2
Stockwell La	15 F3
Stoke Rd	15 A2
Stonecroft Clo	15 B2
Streamside	15 C2
Sunnycroft Clo	15 D3
Sweetbriar Clo	15 B2
Thatchers End	15 E3
The Cloisters	15 B2
The Cornfield	15 A2
The Highgrove	15 B3
The Nurseries	15 B4
The Rowans	15 E3
The Withers	15 C2
Tobyfield Clo	15 D3
Tobyfield La	15 D2
Tobyfield Rd	15 D2
Two Hedges Rd	15 C3
Vilverte Mead	15 A2
Voxwell La	15 B3
Ward Clo	15 D2
Wellbrook Rd	15 C1
Wheatsheaf Dri	15 A2
Whitehouse Way	15 E3
Willcox Dri	15 E3
Willow Clo	15 E3
Willow Park Dri	15 C2
Withyfield Rd	15 B2
Woodmancote Vale	15 E2
Woodmans Way	15 D3
Woodstanway Clo	15 B2
Yarlington Clo	15 B2

BLAKENEY

Name	Ref
All Saints Rd	14 D4
Awre Rd	14 D5
Blakeney Hill Rd	14 A5
Blakeney Hill Rd	14 C5
Bridge St	14 D5
Butts La	14 D5
Chapel Rd	14 A6
Church Sq	14 D5
Church Walk	14 A6
Church Way	14 D5
Cinderford Rd	14 C4
Clarks La	14 C5
Furnace Valley	14 B5
High St	14 C5
Highfield	14 C5
Loiterpin	14 C4
Meadow Clo	14 A6
Mill End	14 D5
New Rd	14 C5
Orchard Gate	14 C5
Pigeon Green	14 A5
Pine Tree Way	14 A6
Pollards La	14 B6
The Smithy	14 D5
Viney Woodside	14 B6

BOURTON-ON-THE-WATER

Name	Ref
Baines Clo	16 B3
Bow La	16 C3
Broadlands Ct	16 D3
Cemetery La	16 C3
Chardwar Gdns	16 C3
Clapton Row	16 C3
Dilker Clo	16 E4
Essex Pl	16 B1
Folly Field	16 C2
Fosse Way	16 A3
Foxes Clo	16 C2
Gasworks La	16 C3
Gorse Clo	16 E4
Gorse Meadow	16 E4
Green La	16 B2
Greystones La	16 D2
High St	16 C2
Hilcote Dri	16 D4
INDUSTRIAL ESTATES:	
Bourton Ind Park	16 C1
Kings Meadow	16 C1
Lamberts Field	16 D3
Letch Hill Dri	16 C3
Letch La	16 C3
Marshmouth La	16 D4
Melville	16 C1
Moore La	16 D2
Moore Rd	16 C2
Mousetrap La	16 B2
Nethercote Dri	16 D4
Nethercote Farm Dri	16 D4
Old Gloucester Rd	16 A2
Park Farm	16 C1
Pegasus Ct	16 C2
Piece Hedge	16 C2
Pockhill La	16 B3
Rectory La	16 C2
Rissington Rd	16 C3
Roman Way	16 C2
Rye Cres	16 D3
Ryeclose	16 D3
Salmondsbury Cotts	16 C2
Sherborne St	16 C3
Springfield	16 B3
Springvale	16 C1
Station Meadow	16 C1
Station Rd	16 C1
The Avenue	16 D4
The Gorse	16 D4
The Naight	16 B2
Victoria St	16 C3

BREAM

Name	Ref
Acacia Clo	17 D3
Badgers Way	17 D3
Beech Way	17 D3
Blue Rock Cres	17 D3
Bowson Rd	17 D1
Bowson Sq	17 D2
Bream Av	17 A3
Brockhollands Rd	17 D3
Coleford Rd	17 A3
Coxs Way	17 D2
Forest Rd	17 D2
Greenacre	17 D4
Hang Hill Rd	17 C2
Henley Rd	17 D2
High St	17 C3
Highbeech Rd	17 C3
Highbury Est	17 C3
Highbury Rd	17 C3
Highview Way	17 D3
Hillside Clo	17 D3
Hillside Est	17 D2
Ironstone Clo	17 C4
Knockley Patch	17 D1
Knox Rd	17 F4
Lansdown Walk	17 D3
Lydney Rd	17 C4
Maypole Green	17 C4
Montpelier Clo	17 E2
Montpelier Rd	17 E3
New Rd, Bream	17 B3
New Rd, Whitecroft	17 F1
Oakley Way	17 C4
Oakwood Rd	17 C2
Parawell La	17 A4
Park Gro	17 F2
Park Hill	17 F2
Parkend Rd	17 D1
Pastors Hill	17 D3
Pillowell Rd	17 F2
Pine Crest Way	17 C3
Puzzle Clo	17 C3
Ryelands Rd	17 C3
Sun Green Clo	17 C3
Sun Green Rd	17 C3
Sun Rise Rd	17 C2
Sun Tump	17 C3
The Tufts	17 B3
Trenchard Rd	17 D4
Whitechapel Rd	17 D2
Whitecroft Rd	17 D2
Whittington Way	17 D4
Woodland Rd	17 C2
Woodlands Clo	17 F2

BROCKWORTH

Name	Ref
Abbotswood Rd	24 B6
Ansdell Dri	24 B4
Astor Clo	24 A4
Astridge Rd	24 D6
Avon Cres	24 C2
Boverton Av	24 B5
Boverton Dri	24 A4
Bryerland Rd	24 D3
Buckholt Way	24 B3
Castle Hill Dri	24 C6
Cedar Rd	24 A4
Chandos Dri	24 B6
Cirencester Rd	24 C6
Clyde Rd	24 B5
Coopers View	24 B6
Court Rd	24 B5
Derwent Clo	24 B5
Elm Dri	24 A4
Ermin Park	24 A4
Ermin St	24 A5
Fairhaven Av	24 B5
Gannet Clo	24 B6
Gladiator Clo	24 A5
Golf Club La	24 A5
Green Acre	24 B6
Green Bank	24 B6
Green Clo	24 B3
Green Gdns	24 B6
Green La	24 D4
Green St	24 A6
Green Way	24 A3
Guise Av	24 B5
Hebden Clo	24 C6
Hickley Gdns	24 C5
Hillview Av	24 B4
Humber Pl	24 A5
Hurcombe Way	24 C5
Javelin Way	24 B4
Lasne Cres	24 B6
Lea Rd	24 C6
Leadon Clo	24 C6
Maple Dri	24 A4
Medway Cres	24 C5
Meteor Way	24 B6
Mill La	24 B5
Mill Cnr	24 D6

MOORFIELD (cont.)

Name	Ref
Moorfield Rd	24 B5
Noak Rd	24 A4
Oak Dri	24 A5
Painswick Rd	24 C6
Pillcroft Clo	24 D6
Pillcroft Rd	24 D6
Pound Clo	24 B6
Ribble La	24 C5
Ridgemount Clo	24 B5
Rowan Gdns	24 A4
St Annes Clo	24 B5
St Georges Rd	24 B6
Sayers Cres	24 B5
Seabrook Rd	24 B6
Shurdington Rd	24 C6
Tamar Rd	24 C5
Tanners Clo	24 B4
The Crescent	24 A4
Theyer Clo	24 B6
Tone Dri	24 C6
Trent Rd	24 C5
Usk Way	24 C6
Vicarage La	24 B5
Westfield Av	24 A4
Westfield Rd	24 A5
Wye Rd	24 C6

CAM/DURSLEY

Name	Ref
Acacia Dri	18 D4
Addymore Clo	18 B3
Ash Clo	18 D4
Beechwood Rise	19 C6
Beyon Clo	18 B2
Beyon Dri	18 B2
Birch Rd	18 C4
Blackboys	19 C5
Blackwells	19 E8
Boulton La	19 D7
Bowers Lea	18 B2
Bramble Dri	18 C4
Broadmere	18 A4
Broadmere Clo	18 A4
Broadwell	19 E7
Broadwell Ter	19 E7
Bull Pitch	19 E7
Burnt Oak	19 C6
Byron Rd	19 E8
Cam Green	18 E2
Cam Pitch	18 B3
Cambridge Av	19 E8
Castle St	19 D6
Cedar Dri	19 D6
Chapel St	18 C2
Church Rd	18 D4
Courthouse Gdns	18 C2
Delkin Rd	18 B3
Drake La	19 E6
Draycott Cres	18 B1
Dursley Rd	18 A4
Elm Lodge	18 D3
Elstub La	18 A3
Everlands	18 C3
Everside Clo	18 B1
Everside La	18 B1
Ewelme Clo	19 F7
Fairmead	18 C3
Ferney	19 E7
Field La	18 A2
Field La	18 A4
First Av	19 E7
Five Acres	19 D7
Fort Fields	19 D7
Fort La	19 E7
Fourth Av	19 F7
Frederick Thomas Rd	18 B3
Ganzell La	19 F8
Glebe Clo	18 C3
Green St	18 E2
Hadley Rd	18 A3
Hague Av	18 B3
Halmore La	18 E1
Hardings Dri	19 D6
Henlow Dri	19 D7
Hermitage Dri	19 E8
Hicks Av	18 B3
High Furlong	18 B3
High St	18 C2
Highfields App	19 E7
Hill Clo	18 C3
Hill Rd	19 C7
Hill Top Vw	18 B3
Holywell Rd	18 C4
Hopton Rd	18 D3
Hunger Hill	19 D7
INDUSTRIALESTATES:	
Draycott Business Park	18 C1
Jubilee Av	18 B1
Jubilee Clo	18 B1
Jubilee Rd	19 C5
Kings Dri	19 C5
Kings Way	19 C5
Kingsdown	19 D5
Kingshill La	19 C5
Kingshill Park	19 C5
Kingshill Rd	19 C5
Kipling Rd	19 F8
Knapp La	18 B2
Lansdowne	18 B4
Larkrise	18 B3
Lawrence Gro	19 C5
Leaside Clo	18 C3
Long St	19 D6
Lower Poole Rd	19 D7
Manor Av	18 B2
Manor Clo	18 B2
Maple Dri	18 C4
Marlestone Rd	18 C4
Marment Rd	18 A4
May Evans Clo	18 B3
May La	19 D7
Meadow Vale	18 B4
Mill Way	18 C3
Millbank	18 D3
Morris Orchard	18 B2
Nasse Ct	18 B2
New Rd	18 B4
Nordown Clo	18 C3
Nordown Rd	18 C3
Norman Hill	18 B3
Nunnery La	19 D8
Oak Dri	18 D4
Old Ct	19 E5
Olive Gro	19 C5
Orchard Clo	18 C3
Orchard Leaze	18 A4
Orchard Rise	18 C4
Park Clo	19 D7
Park La	19 A8
Parkland Rd	18 C4
Parsonage St	19 D6
Pevelands	18 B2
Phillimore Rd	18 A4
Quarry Gdns	18 A4
Rangers Av	19 E8
Rednock Dri	19 D6
Reine Barnes Clo	19 E7
Rock Rd	18 A4
Rosebank	19 D6
Roseberry Mt	19 E7
Roseberry Park	19 E8
Roseberry Rd	19 C5
Rowan Gro	18 D4
Rowley	18 C2
Ryder Clo	18 C4
St Bartholomews Clo	19 C5
St Davids Cres	19 C5
St Georges Clo	18 D4
St Georges Rd	18 C4
School Rd	19 F7
Second Av	19 E7
Severn Rd	18 B4
Shakespeare Rd	19 F8
Shelley Rd	19 F8
Shutehay Dri	18 B2
Silver St	19 D7
Somerset Av	19 E8
Spark Hill	18 B2
Spouthouse La	18 C3
Springfield	18 B4
Springfield Ct	18 B4
Springhill	19 E5
Stanthill Dri	19 E7
Station Rd	18 C3
Steps Clo	18 B2
Stonelea	18 A4
Sutton Clo	18 B3
Tennyson Rd	19 E8
The Avenue	18 A4
The Broadway	19 C7
The Close	18 B3
The Corriet	18 C3
The Crapen	18 A3
The Crescent	18 C2
The Croft	18 C3
The Drive	18 B3
The Hawthorns	18 B3
The Knapp	18 C2
The Quarry	18 A4
The Slade	18 C3
The Vennings	18 C1
Third Av	19 E7
Tilnor Cres	18 C4
Tilsdown	18 B3
Tilsdown Clo	18 B4
Tithe Ct	18 B2
Torchacre Rise	19 C6
Trotman Av	18 B3
Turner Rd	18 A3
Twinberrow La	19 E8
Tyndale Rd	18 A3
Uley Rd	19 E7
Union St	18 B4
Upper Poole Rd	19 D7
Upthorpe	18 B4
Upthorpe La	18 E2
Valley View	18 C3
Vizard Clo	19 E7
Water St	19 E6
Weavers Clo	19 D7
West End	18 A3
Westfield	19 C6
Whiteway	19 F8
Whiteway Clo	19 E8
Willow Clo	18 D4
Windsor Rd	19 D6
Withy Way	18 B3
Woodend La	18 A1
Woodfield Rd	18 A4
Woodland Av	19 C5
Woodland Dri	19 C6
Woodmancote	19 E7
Woodview Rd	18 C3
Wordsworth Rd	19 F8
Yellowhundred Clo	19 E7
Yewtree Clo	18 A4

CHALFORD

Name	Ref
Abbenesse	20 D3
Abnash	20 D3
Ashley Dri	20 B3
Aston View	21 E3
Beale Clo	20 C3
Beech La	20 B4
Beechwood Dri	20 C3
Belvedere Mews	20 C5
Bisley Rd	21 H1
Brantwood Rd	21 E4
Brockley Acres	20 D1
Browns Hill	20 B4
Brownshill Rd	20 B4
Burcombe Rd	20 D3
Burcombe Way	21 E3
Burleigh View	20 B3
Bussage Hill	20 B4
Butts Hill	21 H3
Chapel Hill	21 H2
Chasewood Corner	20 C3
Churchill Rd	20 A5
Cirencestor Rd	21 F6
Commercial Rd	20 D4
Coppice Hill	21 E4
Cotswold Clo	20 A5
Court View	21 E3
Cowcombe Hill	21 E5
Cowswell La	20 B3
Dark La	20 D4
Dr Crouches Rd	20 C1
Dr Middleton Rd	21 E4
Dorrington Ct	21 E3
Down View	21 E3
Eastcombe Rd	20 D2
Farm La	21 H3
Farmcote Clo	20 C2
Farriers Croft	20 C2
Ferris Court View	20 C2
Fidges La	20 D1
Foxes Clo	20 C2
Freame Clo	20 C3
Frithwood	20 C3
Frithwood Clo	20 C4
Frithwood Park	20 C4
Gardiner Clo	20 D2
Greys Clo	20 C2
Gypsy La	21 F6
Haywards La	21 E4
Hidcote Clo	20 C2
High St	20 D5
Highfield Way	21 E3
Hillside	21 F3
Hilltop View	20 C3
INDUSTRIAL ESTATES:	
Chalford Ind Est	20 D5

Street	Ref
Keble Rd	21 E4
Knapp La	20 A6
London Rd	20 A5
Lynch Rd	21 E4
Lypiatt View	20 B2
Marle Hill	20 D5
Marley La	21 F5
Middle Hill	20 D2
Middle Hill Clo	20 D3
Midway	20 D3
Moons La	21 G1
Munday Clo	20 C2
Old Neighbourhood	20 C4
Padin Clo	20 D3
Puddeny Pie La	21 E4
Queens Sq	21 E4
Randalls Grn	21 E4
St Francis La	21 H2
Sezincote Clo	20 C2
Sibtree Clo	20 B3
Silver St	20 D4
Skaiteshill	20 C5
Smythe Meadow	20 B5
Squires Clo	20 B3
Stonecote Ridge	20 C2
Stony Riding	21 E4
Sturmyes Rd	21 F3
Tanglewood Way	20 B3
The Avenue	20 B4
The Birches	21 H2
The Broadway	21 H2
The Bunch of Nuts	21 E4
The Chestnuts	20 B4
The Crescent	21 H2
The Frith	20 C3
The Green	20 C1
The Hawthorns	20 B3
The Old Common	20 C3
The Pitch	20 B4
The Ridge	20 B2
The Ridgeway	20 B3
The Street	20 C1
The Weavers	21 E4
Toadsmoor Rd	20 A5
Tylers Way	21 E3
Upper Lynch Rd	21 E3
Valley Clo	20 A5
Vatch La	20 B2
Velhurst Dri	20 B3
Wells La	20 C1
Windermere	20 D3
Youngs Orchard	20 A5

CHELTENHAM

Street	Ref
Acacia Clo	23 E2
Addis Rd	22 A3
Aggs Hill	23 H6
Albemarle Gate	22 C3
Albert Dri	22 D2
Albert Pl	22 D5
Albert Rd	22 D4
Albert St	22 C4
Albion Pl	22 C5
Albion St	22 C5
Aldridge Clo	22 B4
Alexandra La Walk	23 F4
All Saints Rd	22 D5
All Saints Ter	23 E5
All Saints Villas Rd	22 D5
Alstone Av	22 A5
Alstone Croft	22 A5
Alstone La	22 A5
Ambrose St	22 B5
Anlaby Ct	22 D4
Ann Goodridge Clo	23 G3
Apple Clo	23 E2
Apple Orchard	23 E2
Ariel Lodge Rd	23 E5
Arkle Clo	22 B2
Arle Av	22 A4
Arle Clo	22 A4
Arle Rd	22 A4
Ashley Rd	23 F6
Avon Rd	23 F5
Back Albert Pl	22 D5
Baker St	22 B4
Ballinode Clo	22 A2
Bath Par	22 C6
Bath Rd	22 C6
Bath St	22 C6
Battledown App	23 E6
Battledown Clo	23 E6
Battledown Mead	23 F5
Battledown Priors	23 E6
Baynam Way	22 C5

Street	Ref
Bayshill La	22 B6
Bayshill Rd	22 B6
Beech Clo	23 H3
Beechurst Av	23 E5
Beechwood Clo	23 F6
Belmont Rd	22 D5
Bennington St	22 C5
Berkeley Pl	22 D6
Berkeley St	22 D6
Blackberry Field	23 G4
Blacksmiths La	23 G3
Bloomsbury St	22 B4
Boulton Rd	22 B2
Bouncers La	23 F4
Bowbridge La	23 F2
Bowen Clo	23 F3
Bramble Rise	23 G4
Bredon Walk	23 F4
Briar Walk	23 G4
Bridge St	22 A3
Brighton Rd	22 D6
Broadway Clo	23 F2
Brunswick St	22 C4
Brymore Clo	23 F2
Bullingham Ct	22 B3
Burma Av	23 F5
Burton St	22 B5
Bush Ct	23 F4
Buttercross La	23 H4
Cakebridge Pl	23 E4
Cakebridge Rd	23 E3
Cam Rd	23 F4
Cambray Pl	22 C6
Camp Rd	23 G6
Capel Ct	23 F2
Carlton Pl	22 B4
Carlton St	22 D6
Central Cross Dri	22 D4
Central Way	22 A4
Charles St	22 B4
Chapel Walk	22 B6
Chaple St	22 B5
Chelt Rd	23 F4
Cheviot Rd	23 F3
Chiltern Rd	23 F3
Chosen View Rd	22 A2
Christ Church Rd	22 A6
Churn Av	23 F5
Clarence Rd	22 C4
Clarence Rd	22 C4
Clarence Sq	22 C4
Clarence St	22 C5
Clarington Mws	22 C4
Cleeve Cloud La	23 H3
Cleeve View Rd	23 E5
Cleeveland St	22 B4
Cleevelands Av	22 C2
Cleevelands Clo	22 C2
Cleevelands Dri	22 C2
Cleevemont	22 C2
Cleevemount Clo	23 E3
Cleevemount Rd	23 E3
Clyde Cres	23 F4
Cobham Rd	22 A4
Cobhams Ct	22 A4
College Rd	22 C5
Colletts Dri	22 A4
Colne Av	23 E4
Columbia St	22 A3
Compton Rd	22 A3
Corfe Clo	23 G3
Coronation Rd	23 F3
Cotswold Rd	23 F4
Cottage Rake Av	22 B2
County Court Rd	22 A4
Court Rd	23 G3
Courtenay St	22 C4
Crabtree Pl	22 B4
Cranham Rd	23 E6
Crescent Pl	22 C5
Crescent Ter	22 C5
Cromwell Rd	23 E4
Culross Clo	22 D3
Cumming St	23 F2
Dart Rd	23 F4
Deep St	23 G3
Devonshire St	22 B5
Distel Clo	22 B3
Dorrincourt Mws	22 A5
Douro Rd	22 B6
Drakes Pl	22 A6
Drayton Clo	22 A1
Duke St	22 D6
Dunalley Par	22 C4
Dunalley St	22 C4
East Approach Dri	22 D3
Eldon Av	23 E6
Eldon Rd	23 E5

Street	Ref
Eldorado Rd	22 A6
Elm Clo, Prestbury	23 F2
Elm Clo, St Peters	22 A3
Elm St	22 A3
Elmfield Av	22 B3
Elmfield Rd	22 A3
Evenlode Rd	23 E4
Evesham Rd	22 D1
Fairview Clo	22 D5
Fairview Rd	22 D5
Fairview St	22 D5
Fauconberg Rd	22 B6
Fawley Dri	23 G3
Finchcroft Ct	23 H3
Finchcroft La	23 H3
Fir Tree Clo	23 F3
Florida Dri	23 G3
Folly La	22 B4
Fortina Clo	22 B1
Foxgrove Dri	23 F6
Gallops La	23 H3
Gardeners La	22 A3
Glebe Rd	23 F3
Glenfall St	22 D5
Gloucester Pl	22 D5
Gloucester Rd	22 A5
Golden Miller Rd	22 B2
Goodwin Clo	23 E5
Granville St	22 B4
Gravel Pit La	23 H2
Great Western Rd	22 A5
Great Western Ter	22 B5
Greenway La	23 G6
Grosvenor Pl St	22 D5
Grosvenor St	22 D6
Grosvenor Ter	22 D6
Grove St	22 B5
Hales Clo	23 E5
Hales Rd	23 E6
Hanover St	22 B4
Harp Hill	23 F5
Hayes Rd	23 E5
Haywards La	23 E6
Hendre Mws	22 A5
Henrietta St	22 C5
Hereford Pl	22 B4
Hewlett Pl	22 D6
Hewlett Rd	22 D6
High St, Cheltenham	22 C5
High St, Prestbury	23 G2
Hill Top Rd	22 C2
Hill View Rd	23 F5
Hillcourt Rd	22 D2
Hine Gdns	23 E4
Honeysuckle Clo	23 G4
Hope St	22 A3
Hopwood Gro	23 E5
Hudson St	22 B3
Humber Rd	23 F5
Hungerford St	22 C4
Huntsfield Clo	22 D3
Imjin Rd	23 F5
Imperial La	22 C6
Imperial Sq	22 B6
INDUSTRIAL ESTATES:	
Cheltenham Ind Pk	22 A4
Isbourne Rd	23 F5
Ivy Bank	23 G3
Jersey Av	23 E5
Jersey St	22 D5
Jessop Av	22 B5
Kerstin Clo	22 B2
Kimberley Walk	23 G5
King St	22 B5
Kings Rd	23 E6
Knapp Rd	22 B5
Ladysmith Rd	23 G4
Lake St	23 F2
Landor Gdns	23 E5
Lansdown Cres	22 A6
Lansdown Par	22 A6
Lansdown Terrace La	22 B6
Larput Pl	22 C4
Laurel Dri	23 F2
Leighton Rd	23 D6
Limber Hill	22 B2
Lime Clo	23 E2
Linden Av	23 E2
Linden Clo	23 F2
Linwell Clo	22 A2
Little Cleevemount	22 D3
London Rd	22 D6
Lower Mill St	22 A4
Lynworth Pl	23 F4
Malden Rd	22 D6
Malthouse La	22 C4
Malvern Pl	22 A6
Malvern Rd	22 A5

Street	Ref
Malvern St	22 A3
Mandarin Way	22 A2
Manser St	22 B3
Margrett Rd	22 B4
Market St	22 B4
Marle Hill Par	22 C4
Marle Hill Rd	22 C4
Marsh Clo	22 B3
Marsh Dri	22 B3
Marsh Gdns	22 B3
Marsh La	22 B3
Marston Rd	22 D3
Medoc Clo	22 A2
Mendip Clo	23 E4
Mendip Rd	23 E4
Mersey Rd	23 F5
Midwinter Av	22 B3
Midwinter Clo	22 B2
Mill House Dri	22 B2
Mill La, Ham	23 H6
Mill La, Prestbury	23 H2
Mill St	23 F2
Millbrook Gdns	22 A5
Millbrook St	22 A5
Milsom St	22 B4
Mitre St	22 C6
Monica Dri	22 C3
Monson Av	22 C5
Montpellier Av	22 B6
Montpellier Spa Rd	22 B6
Montpellier St	22 B6
Montpellier Walk	22 B6
Moor Court Dri	23 E5
Morningside Clo	23 G2
Morningside Ct Yd	23 G2
Morris Hill Clo	22 A1
Muscroft Rd	23 H3
New Barn Av	23 F2
New Barn Clo	23 F2
New Barn La	22 D2
New Rutland Ct	22 C5
New St	22 B5
Normal Ter	22 B5
North Hall Mew	23 E5
North Pl	22 C5
North St	22 C5
Noverton Av	23 H3
Noverton La	23 H3
Oak Manor Dri	23 E5
Oakland Av	23 E3
Oakley Rd	23 F6
Old Millbrook Ter	22 A5
Oriel Rd	22 C6
Ormond Pl	22 C6
Overbrook Dri	23 E3
Overton Park Rd	22 B5
Overton Rd	22 A6
Oxford Clo	22 D6
Oxford Par	22 D6
Oxford Pass	22 C5
Oxford St	22 D6
Paddocks La	22 C2
Parabola Clo	22 B6
Parabola La	22 B6
Parabola Rd	22 B6
Park La	23 F1
Park St	22 B5
Pates Av	22 A5
Pendil Clo	22 A1
Pennine Rd	23 F3
Pentathlon Way	22 B2
Piccadilly Way	23 H3
Pittville Circus	22 D4
Pittville Circus Rd	23 E5
Pittville Ct	22 D3
Pittville Cres	22 D4
Pittville Crescent La	22 D4
Pittville Lawn	22 D4
Pittville St	22 C5
Poole Way	22 B4
Popes Clo	22 B4
Portland Sq	22 D5
Portland St	22 C5
Post Office La	22 C5
Prescott Walk	23 F3
Prestbury Green Dri	23 G3
Prestbury Rd	23 E4
Princes St	23 E6
Priors Rd	23 F5
Priory Pl	22 D6
Priory St	22 D6
Priory Ter	22 D6
Priory Walk	22 D6
Promenade	22 B6
Prospect Ter	22 D5
Purbeck Way	23 G3
Queen St	22 A4
Queens Retreat	22 A5

Street	Ref
Queenwood Gro	23 H2
Red Rower Clo	22 B1
Regent St	22 C6
Richards Rd	22 A3
Richmond Dri	23 F5
Roberts Rd	23 H4
Robins Clo	23 E4
Rodney Rd	22 C6
Roman Hackle Av	22 B2
Roman Hackle Rd	22 B2
Rose & Crown Pass	22 C5
Royal Cres	22 C5
Royal Par Mews	22 B6
Royal Well La	22 B6
Royal Well Pl	22 B6
Royal Well Rd	22 C6
Rushy Mws	23 F3
Russel Pl	22 B4
Russel St	22 B4
Sackville App	22 C3
St Annes Clo	22 D5
St Annes Rd	22 D6
St Annes Ter	22 D5
St Arvens Ct	22 D3
St Georges Clo	22 A5
St Georges Dri	22 A5
St Georges Pl	22 B6
St Georges Rd	22 A5
St Georges St	22 C5
St James Sq	22 B5
St James St	22 D6
St Johns Av	22 D6
St Lukes Pl	22 C6
St Margarets Rd	22 C5
St Nicholas Dri	22 C2
St Pauls La	22 B4
St Pauls Rd	22 B4
St Pauls St Nth	22 C4
St Pauls St Sth	22 B5
Salamanca	23 G5
Sandford St	22 C6
Saville Clo	22 D3
Selkirk Clo	22 D4
Selkirk Gdns	22 D4
Selkirk St	22 D5
Seneca Way	22 A2
Seven Posts All	23 F3
Severn Rd	23 E4
Shaw Green La	23 F1
Sherborne Pl	22 D5
Sherbourn	22 D5
Sidney St	22 D6
Somme Rd	23 F4
South View Way	23 G3
Southam Rd	23 G1
Spring La	23 F1
Stanley Rd	23 F6
Stanwick Cres	22 A2
Stanwick Dri	22 A2
Stanwick Gdns	22 A3
Station St	22 B5
Stirling Ct	22 A4
Stoneville St	22 B4
Studland Dri	23 G3
Sun St	22 A4
Swindon Clo	22 B4
Swindon La	22 A1
Swindon Rd	22 A4
Swindon St	22 B4
Sydenham Rd Nth	23 E6
Sydenham Rd Sth	23 E6
Sydenham Villas Rd	22 D6
Tamar Rd	23 E4
Tatchley La	23 F3
Teme Rd	23 E5
Tewkesbury Rd	22 A3
Thames Rd	23 E4
The Bank	23 G2
The Burgage	23 F2
The Conifers	23 E4
The Gardens	22 D3
The Grove, Cheltenham	23 E6
The Grove, Lansdown	22 A6
The Gryphons	23 E5
The Spinney	22 D2
The Stables	23 H2
The Strand	22 C6
Thomond Clo	22 A2
Thornbury Co	22 A5
Three Sisters La	23 H3
Tilney Rd	22 C2
Tom Price Clo	22 D5
Tommy Taylors La	22 B3
Townsend St	22 B4
Trafalgar St	22 C6
Trinity La	22 C5

Trinity School La 22 D5
Union St 22 D5
Upper Mill La 23 H2
Vernon Pl 22 C6
Victoria Pl 22 D5
Victoria St 22 B4
Victoria Ter 23 E6
Vine Ct 22 B4
Vittoria Walk 22 C6
Waddon Dri 23 E4
Walnut Clo 22 D3
Warwick Pl 22 C5
Waterloo St 22 A3
Watershoot Clo 23 E2
Well Pl 22 A6
Welland Ct 23 E3
Welland Dri 23 E3
Welland Lodge Rd 23 E3
Wellesley Rd 22 C4
Wellington Rd 22 D4
Wellington St 22 C6
Wellington Sq 22 C4
Wendover Gdns 22 A6
Wessex Dri 23 F5
West Approach Dri 22 D3
West Down Gdns 22 D5
West Dri 22 C4
Westbourne Dri 23 E5
Western Rd 22 A5
Westwood La 23 H4
Whaddon Av 23 E5
Whaddon Rd 23 E4
White Hart St 22 B4
Whitethorne Dri 23 G4
Willow Rd 23 F6
Willowherb Clo 23 G4
Winchcombe St 22 C5
Windrush Rd 23 F5
Windsor St 22 D4
Windyridge Gdns 22 B2
Windyridge Rd 22 A2
Winstonian Rd 22 D5
Witcombe Pl 22 D6
Worcester St 22 A3
Wymans La 22 A2
Wymans Rd 23 E4
Yew Tree Clo 22 B2
York Row 23 F3
York St 22 D5

CHIPPING CAMPDEN

Aston Rd 24 B1
Back Ends 24 B2
Badgers Field 24 B2
Berrington Rd 24 D2
Blind La 24 A3
Calfs La 24 B2
Castle Gdns 24 D2
Catbrook Clo 24 B3
Cherry Orchard Clo 24 B3
Church St 24 C2
Cidermill La 24 C1
Coldicotts Clo 24 B2
Conduit Hill 24 A3
Coneygree Fold 24 C2
Coronation Clo 24 A2
Dyers La 24 A2
George La 24 B3
Grafton Mews 24 B2
Grevel La 24 B1
Griggs Clo 24 B1
Haydens Clo 24 C1
Haysums Clo 24 B3
High St 24 B2
Hoo La 24 A2
Izods Clo 24 B3
Kingcombe La 24 A1
Leysbourne 24 B2
Littleworth 24 A2
Lower High St 24 B2
Neighbridge Ct 24 C1
Park Rd 24 A3
Pear Tree Clo 24 B3
Poplars Clo 24 A3
Rolling Stones 24 B2
Seymour Gate 24 B2
Sheep St 24 B3
Station Rd 24 C1
The Green 24 B3
Westend Ter 24 B2
Wolds End Clo 24 B1

CINDERFORD

Abbey St 25 C2
Abbots Rd 25 D3
Albert Rd 25 B3
Albion Rd 25 C1
Ashdean 25 B1
Ashmead Rd 25 D3
Barleycorn Sq 25 B2
Beacons View Rd 25 D2
Beech Way 25 F2
Beechdean 25 B1
Belle Vue Rd 25 C2
Bilson 25 B1
Birchwood Clo 25 A1
Broad St 25 E3
Brookside Rd 25 A1
Buckshaft Rd 25 C4
Cartway Grn 25 B2
Causeway Rd 25 C1
Church Rd 25 B4
Church St 25 F3
Church Walk 25 F3
College Rd 25 C2
Commercial St 25 C2
Coomb Dri 25 C4
Crabtree Rd 25 A1
Crawshay Pl 25 B2
Danby Clo 25 D2
Dean Cres 25 F3
Dockham Rd 25 C2
Double View 25 C3
Edge Hills Clo 25 C2
Edge Hills Rd 25 C2
Elmdean 25 B1
Elton Rd 25 F2
Fairfields 25 B2
Ferndale Clo 25 D1
Flaxley St 25 C3
Forest Rise 25 D1
Forest Road 25 C2
Forest Vale Rd 25 A1
Foxes Bridge Rd 25 B2
Furnaces Clo 25 B2
George La 25 E3
Greenhill Clo 25 D1
Greenway Rd 25 B4
Hastings Rd 25 B2
Hazeldean 25 B1
Heywood Rd 25 C2
High St, Cinderford 25 B1
High St, Littledean 25 E2
Highview Rd 25 D3
Hollydean 25 B2
Hollyhill Rd 25 A1

INDUSTRIAL ESTATES:
Forest Vale Ind Est 25 B2
Station View
  Business Pk 25 B2
Kensley Vale 25 B3
Lamb La 25 C2
Lantern Clo 25 B2
Latimer Rd 25 D1
Laymore Rd 25 A1
Littledeanhill Rd 25 D3
Mapledean 25 B1
Market St 25 C2
Meadow Rd 25 D2
Meendhurst Rd 25 C3
Miners Walk 25 B2
Moorland Clo 25 D1
Mount Pleasant Rd 25 D3
Mountjoys La 25 C1
Mountjoys La End 25 C1
Mousel La 25 C3
Northwood Clo 25 C1
Oak Way 25 F2
Oakdean 25 B1
Oakwood Clo 25 D1
Office Rd 25 B3
Packers Rd 25 C2
Parragate 25 C1
Parragate Rd 25 B1
Pembroke St 25 C2
Pinewood Clo 25 D1
Prospect Rd 25 C2
Reddings La 25 D2
Roman Way 25 C1
Rowandean 25 B1
Ruspidge Rd 25 D2
St Annals Rd 25 D2
St Johns Sq 25 B4
St Whites Rd 25 B4
Seven Stars Rd 25 B1

Severn View 25 D2
Silver St 25 F3
Somerset Rd 25 B2
Southwood Clo 25 C1
Springfield Dri 25 C1
Station St 25 B2
Station Ter 25 B2
Stockwell Grn 25 C3
Sutton Rd 25 E3
The Buffit 25 E1
The Keelings 25 B2
The Oakfield 25 D2
Trinity Way 25 C1
Upper Bilson Rd 25 B1
Valley Rd 25 B2
Victoria Clo 25 B3
Victoria St 25 B3
Victoria Vale 25 C2
Wesley Rd 25 C2
West View 25 C3
Westerley Clo 25 C3
Westfield Ct 25 C1
Westfield Rd 25 C1
Willowdean 25 B1
Woodgate Rd 25 C1
Woodlands Rd 25 C3
Woodside Av 25 C3
Woodside St 25 C2
Woodside St 25 C2
Woodville Rd 25 D3
Worcester Rd 25 D2
York Rd 25 D2

CIRENCESTER

Abbey Way 26 B4
Abbots Rd 27 E5
Akeman Rd 27 E5
Albion St 26 B3
Alexander Dri 27 C7
Apsley Clo 27 B7
Apsley Rd 27 B7
Archery Rd 26 E4
Arnolds Way 26 E4
Ashcroft Gdns 27 C5
Ashcroft Rd 27 E5
Austin Rd 27 E5
Barn Way 26 A2
Barton La 26 B4
Bathurst Rd 27 B7
Baunton La 26 A1
Beaufort Ct 27 C7
Beech Gro 27 D5
Beeches Rd 27 C8
Berkeley Rd 27 C8
Berry Hill Cres 27 C5
Berry Hill Rd 26 C3
Bishops Walk 27 C5
Black Jack St 27 C5
Blake Rd 26 C4
Blue Quarry Rd 27 E5
Bluebell Dri 27 E8
Bowling Green Av 26 C3
Bowling Green La 26 B4
Bowling Green Rd 26 C3
Bowly Rd 27 B7
Bridge Clo 27 D7
Bridge End 27 D7
Bridge Rd 27 D7
Bristol Rd 27 B6
Brooke Rd 27 B7
Burford Rd 26 E4
Cambray Ct 27 D5
Carpenters La 27 D5
Castle St 27 C5
Cecily Hill 27 B5
Cheltenham Rd 26 B3
Cherry Tree Dri 27 E7
Cherrytree La 26 F3
Chester Cres 27 D6
Chester St 27 D6
Chesterton Gro 27 A6
Chesterton La 27 A6
Chesterton Park 27 A6
Church Av 27 E8
Church St 27 D6
Churchill Rd 27 E5
City Bank Rd 27 D6
Coach House Mews 27 D5
College View 27 B8
Corinium Gate 27 D5
Cotswold Av 27 B6
Cotswold Clo 27 B6
Countess Lilias Rd 27 B7
Coxwell St 27 C5
Crabtree La 27 E6

Cranhams La 27 A7
Cricklade Rd 27 E7
Cricklade Rd 27 C5
Crips Rd 27 C5
Dollar St 26 C4
Donside 26 A2
Drift Clo 27 A7
Drift Way 27 A7
Dugdale Rd 26 C4
Dyer St 27 C5
Edgeworth 27 A7
Elliot Rd 27 D8
Elphick Rd 26 A2
Ermin Pl 27 E7
Esland Rd 27 D7
Estcote Rd 26 C4
Fairfax Clo 27 C7
Fairfax Rd 27 C7
Farrell Clo 27 C5
Fosse Clo 26 E4
Foxes Bank Dri 27 B7
Foxglove Clo 27 E8
Gallows Pound La 26 B2
Garden Clo 27 C6
Gardner Ct 27 D6
*Garland Ct,
  Fairfax Rd 27 C7
Gibson Ct 27 C7
Glebe Clo 26 B2
Gloucester Rd 26 A1
Gloucester St 26 B4
Golden Farm Rd 27 E5
Gooseacre 26 B4
Gooseacre La 26 B4
Gosditch St 27 C5
Grange Ct 26 B1
Grantley Cres 27 C7
Greyfriars Walk 27 B8
Grove La 26 C4
Hakeburn Rd 26 C4
Hammond 27 B5
Hammond Way 27 B6
Hanover Ct 27 D6
Hanstone Clo 27 B7
Haresfield 26 B1
Haygarth Clo 27 B7
Herbert Stalk Clo 27 E5
Hereward Rd 26 C4

INDUSTRIAL ESTATES:
Love La Ind Est 27 D7
The Corinium
  Centre 27 D8
Jobbins Ct 27 C5
Kemble Dri 27 A7
King St 27 D6
Kings Way 27 F7
Kingshill 27 F6
Kingshill La 27 F5
Kingsmead 27 D7
Lavender Ct 27 C6
Lavender La 27 C6
Lawrence Rd 27 B7
Leaholme Ct 27 D6
Lewis La 27 C5
Limes Clo 27 C7
Linacre Cres 27 B8
Links View 26 B1
London Rd 27 D5
Love La 27 D7
Manor Clo 26 B1
Market Pl 27 C5
Martin Clo 27 C6
Masefield 27 B7
Meadow Clo 27 C7
Meadow Rd 27 C7
Mellmore Gdns 27 E7
Mercian Clo 27 D7
Michaels Mead 27 B7
Midland Rd 27 D7
Morestall Dri 27 B7
Mount Clo 27 C6
Mount St 27 C6
Newcombe Ct 27 D5
North Farm Rd 27 F6
North Hill Rd 27 E8
North Home Rd 27 E6
North Way 27 C5
Nursery Clo 27 D7
Oaklands 27 C7
Oakley Rd 27 B7
Overhill Rd 26 A2
Park La 27 B5
Park St 27 B5
Park View 26 B2
Parkland Sq 27 B7
Partridge Way 27 E5
Patterson Rd 27 E5
Pheasant Way 27 E5

Phoenix Way 27 C6
Popes Ct 26 A2
Primrose Way 27 E8
Priory Rd 26 C4
Prospect Pl 27 D7
Purley Av 27 D5
Purley Rd 27 D5
Quarry Clo 26 B2
Queen Annes Rd 27 D5
Queen Elizabeth Rd 27 E6
Queen St 27 D6
Querns La 27 C6
Querns Rd 27 C6
Reeves Clo 27 A7
Rendcomb Dri 27 A7
Roberts Clo 26 B2
Rose Way 27 E7
Rutland Pl 27 C5
St Johns Clo 26 B2
St Johns Rd 26 C4
St Lawrence Clo 26 B4
St Marys Rd 27 C6
St Michaels Rd 27 C6
St Peters Ct 27 C6
St Peters Rd 27 C6
Saxon Rd 27 E5
School Hill 26 A2
School La 27 D6
Shalford Clo 27 B7
Sheep St 27 C5
Shepherds Way 26 C4
Siddington Rd 27 D7
Silver St 27 C5
Smiths Field 27 A6
Somerford Rd 27 C5
Somerville Ct 27 B8
South Way 27 C5
Southgate Mews 27 D6
Southmead 27 E7
Sperrin Gate 27 D6
Spitalgate La 26 C4
Springfield Rd 27 B7
Steepstairs La 27 D6
Stow Rd 26 F1
Stratton Heights 26 B1
Stroud Rd 27 A6
Swindon Rd 27 D5
Tetbury Rd 27 A6
The Avenue 27 C6
The Glade 27 E8
The Green 27 E5
The Green 27 E8
The Maples 27 B8
The Mead 26 B4
The Pyghtell 26 B3
The Smithy 27 E6
The Waterloo 27 D5
The Whiteway 26 C4
Thessaly Rd 26 A1
Thomas St 27 B5
Tinglesfield 26 B2
Tower Ct 27 C5
Tower St 27 C5
Trafalgar Rd 26 B4
Trinity Rd 27 E5
Tudor Rd 27 E5
Upper Chirnside 27 E5
Vaisey Rd 26 A1
Vale Rd 26 B2
Victoria Rd 27 D5
Vyners Clo 27 C7
Watermoor Rd 27 C7
Watermoor Way 27 D7
Weavers Rd 27 E5
West Market St 27 C5
West Way 27 C5
Whitelands Rd 27 E5
Whiteway View 26 B2
Whitwood Rd 27 C6
Wilkinson Rd 27 C8
Windsor Walk 27 A5
Woodhouse Clo 27 B7
Woodlands Rd 27 B7

COLEFORD

Adams Way 28 A2
Albert Rd 28 A5
Ambrose La 28 D4
Angel Field 28 A5
Aston Clo 28 B2
Bakers Hill 28 C4
Bank St 28 A5
Barn Hill Rd 28 D4
Bath Pl 28 B1
Baynhams Walk 28 D3

Orchard Clo	32 B3
Orchard Gdns	32 C3
Orchard Rd	32 B3
Orchard Vale	32 C3
Owls Head Rd	32 B4
Ozleworth	32 D3
Palmers Clo	32 D5
Park Clo	32 B3
Park Rd	32 B2
Park View	32 B3
Parklands	32 B2
Parkwall Rd	32 D6
Parkwell Cress	32 C6
Peacocks La	32 A3
Penard Way	32 C3
Perrot Rd	32 D2
Petherton Clo	32 B3
Pettigrove Gdns	32 B4
Pettigrove Rd	32 B4
Pillingers Rd	32 A3
Pine Wood	32 C1
Pippin Clo	32 C6
Poplar Ter	32 C3
Pound Rd	32 C1
Pows Rd	32 A3
Press Moor Dri	32 C6
Purton Clo	32 B4
Quarry Clo	32 A5
Quarter Mile Alley	32 B1
Queens Rd	32 D6
Regent St	32 A2
Rodborough Way	32 D4
Runnymede	32 B2
Russell Av	32 B4
Russell Ct	32 C3
St Andrews	32 D4
St Davids Av	32 D5
Sassoon Ct	32 D6
School Rd	32 A3
School Rd	32 D6
Scott Ct	32 C6
Selkirk Rd	32 A1
Selworthy	32 B3
Seymour Rd	32 A2
Sherbourne Clo	32 C1
Shilton Clo	32 C3
Shortwood View	32 C2
Siston Common	32 D1
Skippon Ct	32 B6
Somerton Clo	32 B4
Soundwell Rd	32 A2
South Rd	32 A2
Southfield Av	32 B2
Southley Av	32 B2
Spring Hill	32 B1
Stafford Ct	32 D5
Stanton Clo	32 C1
Staverton Way	32 D4
Staynes Cres	32 B2
Stephens Dri	32 C6
Stokes Ct	32 D6
Stone Hill	32 B6
Stoneleigh Dri	32 C5
Stourton Dri	32 C6
Swaish Dri	32 C6
Syston Way	32 A1
Tanner Clo	32 C5
Taylor Clo	32 C2
Tennis Court Rd	32 D1
The Haven	32 B1
The Meadows	32 A6
The Orchards	32 C3
The Park	32 B2
The Ride	32 D1
The Twynings	32 B1
Tibberton	32 D2
Tintern Clo	32 C5
Tippetts Rd	32 A4
Tower Rd	32 A1
Trevethin Clo	32 A4
Troon Dri	32 D4
Turnberry	32 D4
Tyler Clo	32 B5
Tyndale Rd	32 B1
Unity St	32 A2
Victoria Park	32 A2
Victoria Rd	32 A5
Walnut Clo	32 C2
Walnut Dri	32 C2
Walnut La	32 D3
Warner Clo	32 C4
Waters Rd	32 A2
Webb Clo	32 C4
Wedmore Clo	32 C4
Wellington Rd	32 A1
Wentworth	32 D4
Wesley Av	32 A5
Wesley Hill	32 A1

Wesley Hill	32 A1
West St	32 A3
Westfield Clo	32 B6
Westons Way	32 C4
Whitecroft Way	32 A3
Whitefield Av	32 A5
Whittucks Clo	32 A6
Whittucks Rd	32 A6
Willis Rd	32 D1
Wilmot Ct	32 D5
Wilshire Av	32 A5
Witcombe Clo	32 C1
Woburn Clo	32 C5
Wood Rd	32 A3
Woodcote	32 A5
Woodend	32 A4
Woodington Ct	32 C6
Woodland Ter	32 B3
Woodstock	32 C3
Woodstock Clo	32 C3
Woodstock Rd	32 C3
Woody Leaze	32 A5
Woodyleaze Dri	32 A5
Worcester Rd	32 A2
Worth Clo	32 C4
Wraxall Rd	32 D4
Wychwood	32 B4
Wyns Ct	32 B6

LECHLADE

Abbots Walk	33 C2
Bell La	33 B3
Briary Rd	33 C1
Bridge Walk	33 C3
Burford St	33 C2
Butlers Fld	33 B1
Chancel Way	33 C2
Cuthwine Pl	33 B2
Gassons Rd	33 B2
Gassons Way	33 B2
Hambridge La	33 B1
High St	33 B3
Katherines Walk	33 C2
Keble Clo	33 C1
Kingsmead	33 B1
Loders Field	33 B2
Market Pl	33 C3
Mill La	33 D3
Moorgate	33 A2
Oak St	33 C2
Pigeon Clo	33 B3
Roman Way	33 C1
St Birinus Ct	33 C2
St Johns St	33 C3
St Lawrence Rd	33 C2
Shelleys Walk	33 C3
Sherborne St	33 B3
Station Rd	33 C1
Thames St	33 B3
The Cursus	33 B1
The Loders	33 B2
The Spinney	33 B2
West Way	33 C1
Wharf La	33 C3

LEONARD STANLEY/ KINGS STANLEY

Bath Rd	33 A5
Bathleaze	33 C5
Beeches Clo	33 C4
Borough Clo	33 C6
Brimley	33 B5
Broad St	33 C5
Brockley Rd	33 B4
Castle Mead	33 B5
Castle St	33 B6
Church Rd	33 A5
Church St	33 C6
Coldwell	33 D6
Coldwell Clo	33 D6
Coldwell La	33 D6
Coombe La	33 D6
Daffodil Leaze	33 D6
Dozule Clo	33 D6
Elm Clo	33 C4
Elmlea Rd	33 C4
Gardeners Way	33 C4
Guildings Way	33 C4
Gypsy La	33 A6
High St	33 C5
Mankley Rd	33 B5
Marsh La	33 B6

Marsh Rd	33 B5
New St	33 C5
Orchard Clo	33 D6
Penn La	33 D6
St Georges Av	33 C4
St Georges Clo	33 B4
Selwyn Clo	33 C4
Shute St	33 C5
Tannery Clo	33 A5
Tannery Cotts	33 A5
The Luggs	33 C5
The Nursery	33 A5
The Street	33 A5
Wesley Ct	33 A5
Woodlands	33 A5
Woodside La	33 B6

LYDNEY

Albert St	34 B2
Almond Walk	34 B2
Ash Clo	34 B2
Augustus Way	34 C1
Bath Pl	34 B3
Bathurst Park Rd	34 B3
Beauchamp Mdw	34 C2
Beaufort Dri	34 B1
Berkeley Cres	34 B1
Bishops Gate	34 A4
Bracken Clo	34 C3
Bracken Dri	34 C3
Bream Rd	34 A2
Caesars Clo	34 C2
Cambourne Pl	34 C4
Centurion Rd	34 C2
Chantry Clo	34 A5
Charnwood Clo	34 B1
Cherry Walk	34 B2
Church Gdns	34 B4
Church Rd	34 A4
Claudius Way	34 C2
Cookson Ter	34 B6
Crump Pl	34 D4
Darters Clo	34 A4
Dean Ct	34 B1
Driffield Rd	34 C1
Fairfield Rd	34 B3
Forest Rd	34 B2
Greenways	34 A4
Grove Rd	34 A3
Hadrian Clo	34 C2
Hams Rd	34 B3
Harbour Rd	34 B6
Harrison Way	34 C4
High St	34 A4
Highfield La	34 C1
Highfield Rd	34 B3
Hill St	34 B3
Hopes Clo	34 C4
INDUSTRIAL ESTATES:	
Lydney Ind Est	34 D6
Jubilee Rd	34 C3
Julius Way	34 C2
June Dri	34 C1
Kimberley Clo	34 C3
Kimberley Dri	34 C2
Klondyke Av	34 C3
Lakeside Av	34 C4
Lakeside Dri	34 C4
Lancaster Ct	34 B1
Lancaster Dri	34 B1
Lime Way	34 B2
Livia Way	34 C2
Lych Gate	34 A5
Lydfield Rd	34 B3
Lynwood Rd	34 B1
Manor Rd	34 C3
Mead La	34 A6
Meadowbank	34 C1
Minverva Walk	34 C1
Mount Pleasant	34 A3
Naas La	34 B3
Nero Clo	34 C2
New Rd	34 A1
Newerne St	34 A4
Nodens Way	34 C2
Oak Meadow	34 C1
Octavia Pl	34 C2
Old Town Ms	34 A4
Orchard Rd	34 C4
Oxford St	34 A4
Park Ct	34 B3
Primrose Hill Rd	34 B2
Primrose Way	34 B1
Purton Pl	34 D4
Pylers Way	34 C4

Queen St	34 B2
Regent St	34 B3
Ridler Rd	34 C4
Ridley Sq	34 C4
Rodley Rd	34 C3
Rushyleaze	34 C4
Sabrina Way	34 C2
St Marys Sq	34 C3
School Cres	34 B1
Severn Rd	34 C4
Severnbank Av	34 D3
Shepherdine Clo	34 D3
South Rd	34 B2
Spring Meadow Rd	34 B2
Springfield Rd	34 B2
Stanford Rd	34 A3
Station Rd	34 B5
Steel Av	34 C3
Steeple Vw	34 B4
Summer Leaze	34 C4
Summerleaze Rd	34 C4
Swan Rd	34 B3
Temple Clo	34 A3
Templeway	34 A4
Templeway West	34 A3
Tiberius Av	34 C2
The Folders	34 C3
The Orchard	34 A3
The Springs	34 B2
Tutnalls St	34 C3
Valley Rd	34 C4
Vicarage Clo	34 B5
Victoria Rd	34 B3
Whitecross Rd	34 A4
Willow Heights	34 B1
Woodland Rise	34 B2
Wyntours Par	34 A4

MANGOTSFIELD

Acacia Av	35 B6
Acacia Clo	35 B6
Acacia Rd	35 B6
Albert Rd	35 C5
Alexandra Clo	35 C6
Alexandra Gdns	35 C6
Alexandra Pl	35 C6
Almond Way	35 D5
Amberley Clo	35 B2
Amberley Rd	35 B2
Aufori Rd	35 C5
Avon Ring Rd	35 B1
Badminton Rd	35 C3
Baglyn Av	35 D6
Bankside	35 D5
Bath St	35 C5
Baugh Gdns	35 D1
Baugh Rd	35 D1
Beachgrove Gdns	35 A6
Beachgrove Rd	35 A5
Beaufort Pl	35 A1
Beazer Clo	35 C6
Beckspool Rd	35 A1
Beechen Dri	35 B6
Beechwood Rd	35 A6
Benford Clo	35 B4
Berkley Grn	35 A1
Berkley Rd	35 A5
Bexley Rd	35 A6
Boscombe Clo	35 D2
Boscombe Cres	35 D2
Bracey Rd	35 A4
Briar Walk	35 A6
Briar Way	35 A6
Bridgeleap Rd	35 D1
Bristol Rd	35 A1
Broad St	35 C5
Broadoak Wk	35 A6
Bromley Dri	35 C1
Bromley Heath Av	35 C2
Bromley Heath Rd	35 B2
Brook Rd	35 A6
Bryants Clo	35 B1
Buckingham Gdns	35 C4
Buckingham Pl	35 C4
Burley Av	35 D4
Burley Crest	35 D4
Burley Gro	35 D4
Byron Pl	35 C5
Carpenters Shop La	35 C4
Cassell Rd	35 B5
Cave Dri	35 B3
Chapel La	35 A2
Charnhill Cres	35 D6
Charnhill Dri	35 D6
Charnhill Vale	35 D6

Charnwell Rd	35 D5
Chesterfield Rd	35 D4
Chestnut Rd	35 C4
Chewton Clo	35 A6
Chine Vw	35 D2
Christchurch Av	35 C4
Christchurch La	35 C4
Church Av	35 C4
Church La	35 D1
Church Rd	35 A2
Church Vw	35 C4
Clarence Av	35 C5
Clarence Gdns	35 C5
Clarence Rd	35 C5
Cleeve Av	35 C3
Cleeve Ct	35 C3
Cleeve Dale	35 B2
Cleeve Gdns	35 B2
Cleeve Hill	35 C3
Cleeve Hill Ext	35 C3
Cleeve Lawns	35 C3
Cleeve Lodge Clo	35 C3
Cleeve Lodge Rd	35 C3
Cleeve Park Rd	35 C3
Cleeve Rd, Frenchay	35 A1
Cleeve Rd, Mangotsfield	35 C3
Cleeve Wood Rd	35 B2
Cliff Ct Dri	35 A2
Clifford Rd	35 B5
Coggan Rd	35 C6
Conifer Clo	35 B3
Coronation Rd	35 C4
Crescent Rd	35 B1
Croomes Hill	35 B4
Crossfield Rd	35 D6
Crown La	35 C6
Crownleaze	35 C6
Cunningham Gdns	35 A4
Daubeny Clo	35 A4
Delabere Av	35 A4
Dial La	35 C4
Dodisham Dri	35 A4
Downend Pk Rd	35 B5
Downend Rd	35 A5
Downleaze	35 C2
Ducie Rd	35 C5
Eastleigh Clo	35 D6
Eastleigh Rd	35 D6
Eaton Clo	35 A5
Edgeware Rd	35 B5
Edmund Clo	35 B4
Elliot Av	35 B1
Ettrike Dri	35 A4
Fairlyn Dri	35 D6
Farm Ct	35 D3
Farm Rd	35 C3
Field Vw Dri	35 B3
Filton Rd	35 A1
Florence Rd	35 C6
Forest Way	35 A6
Four Acre Av	35 D2
Four Acre Cres	35 D1
Four Acre Rd	35 C1
Frampton Cres	35 B6
Frenchay Clo	35 A3
Frenchay Common	35 A2
Frenchay Hill	35 A2
Frenchay Rd	35 A3
Frome Side Pk	35 A3
Frome Vs	35 A2
Furze Rd	35 B6
Garnett Pl	35 D2
Gerrish Av	35 D5
Gill Av	35 A4
Glendale	35 C1
Glenside Clo	35 A3
Gloucester Rd	35 C6
Goffenton Dri	35 A4
Gorse Hill	35 A6
Grace Rd	35 B5
Graham Rd	35 D3
Grange Dri	35 B4
Grange Pk	35 B4
Grange Wood Clo	35 B4
Greenleaze Av	35 C1
Greenleaze Clo	35 C1
Greystones	35 B2
Grove Bank	35 B1
Halbrow Cres	35 B4
Harford Dri	35 A1
Haynes St	35 B5
Hayward Rd	35 B6
Heath Ct	35 C2
Heath Gdns	35 C2
Heath Rd	35 C2

Heath Wk	35 B2
Heathcote Rd	35 C5
Hermitage Rd	35 C5
High St	35 B5
Hill House Rd	35 D4
Hillfields Av	35 B6
Homestead Gdns	35 A1
Howard Rd	35 B6
Hurstwood Rd	35 B4
Idstone Rd	35 A6
INDUSTRIAL ESTATES:	
Hayward Ind Est	35 B6
Irving Clo	35 C6
James Clo	35 C6
James Rd	35 C6
Jubilee Rd	35 D6
Kelston Wk	35 B6
Kendall Gdns	35 B6
Kendall Rd	35 B6
Kensington Rd	35 B5
Kimberley Av	35 A5
Kimberley Clo	35 D2
Kimberley Cres	35 A5
Kimberley Rd	35 A5
Lanway Rd	35 A4
Lawn Av	35 A5
Lawn Rd	35 A5
Leap Valley Cres	35 D2
Ledbury Rd	35 A5
Lewington Rd	35 A5
Lincombe Av	35 B4
Lincombe Rd	35 B4
Lodge Wk	35 B4
Long Clo	35 A4
Longden Rd	35 D4
Lower Station Rd	35 B5
Lulworth Cres	35 D2
Lychet Dri	35 D2
Lydney Rd	35 C5
Malmains Dri	35 A1
Mangotsfield Rd	35 D5
Manor Pl	35 A1
Marlborough Dri	35 A1
Marshfield Park	35 B2
Marshfield Rd	35 A6
Maywood Av	35 A5
Maywood Cres	35 A5
Maywood Rd	35 A5
Meadow Clo	35 D2
Middle Rd	35 D6
Midland Rd	35 B6
Millward Gro	35 A5
Morley Clo	35 C6
Morley Rd	35 C6
Narrow La	35 C6
Nelson Rd	35 B5
North Vw, Mangotsfield	35 D5
North Vw, Upper Soundwell	35 B6
Northcote Rd	35 D4
Oakdale Av	35 C2
Oakdale Clo	35 C2
Oakdale Ct	35 C2
Oakdale Rd	35 C2
Overdale Rd	35 B4
Overhurst Ct	35 B4
Overnhill Ct	35 B5
Overnhill Rd	35 B4
Page Clo	35 D5
Page Rd	35 B5
Park Cres	35 B1
Park Rd	35 C4
Parkhurst Av	35 A6
Peach Rd	35 D4
Pemberton Ct	35 A5
Pendennis Av	35 B5
Pendennis Rd	35 B5
Pendock Rd	35 A3
Penn Dri	35 B1
Pilgrims Wy	35 C2
Pleasant Rd	35 B5
Portland Pl	35 B6
Portland St	35 B6
Prattens La	35 B5
Quakers Clo	35 C1
Quakers Rd	35 C1
Quarry Rd	35 A2
Queensholme Av	35 C1
Queensholme Clo	35 C1
Queensholme Cres	35 C1
Queensholme Rd	35 C1
Radley Rd	35 A5
Railway Ter	35 B6
Riverside Dri	35 A3
Riverwood Rd	35 B1
Riviera Cres	35 C6
Rockland Rd	35 B3

Rockside Av	35 D1
Rodway Vw	35 D6
Ronayne Wk	35 A4
Rose Wk	35 B6
Rosedale Rd	35 A6
Salisbury Gdns	35 C4
Salisbury Rd	35 C4
Sandholme Clo	35 C2
Sandringham Av	35 C1
Sandringham Pk	35 C2
Saunders Rd	35 C5
Selbrooke Cres	35 A3
Seymour Rd	35 C5
Shepherds Clo	35 C5
Sheppard Rd	35 A4
Shimsey Clo	35 B4
Shrubbery Rd	35 B4
Sidlands Rd	35 B3
Signal Rd	35 D6
Soundwell Rd	35 C6
South Vw	35 D5
Southernhay	35 B6
Stanbury Av	35 A5
Standbridge Clo	35 D4
Standbridge Rd	35 D3
Stanley Pk Rd	35 C6
Staplehill Rd	35 A5
Station Rd	35 D6
Summerleaze	35 B6
Sunridge	35 B4
Sutherland Av	35 D2
Symington Rd	35 A5
Teetwell Av	35 C6
Teetwell Clo	34 C6
Teetwell Hill	35 D5
Tern Rd	35 C5
The Common	35 A2
The Crescent	35 B6
The Crest	35 D4
The Gardens	35 C6
The Park	35 A1
The Rosery	35 A6
Thicket Av	35 A6
Thicket Rd	35 B5
Tuckett La	35 A2
Tylers La	35 B5
Uplands Rd	35 B6
Upper Station Rd	35 B5
Urfords Dri	35 B3
Valley Gdns	35 D2
Victoria North St	35 C5
Wadham St	35 A1
Wedgewood Rd	35 C1
Wellington Dri	35 A1
Wenmore Clo	35 C1
West Park Rd	35 C5
Westbourne Rd	35 D2
Westerleigh Rd	35 D3
White Lodge Rd	35 D6
Whittington Rd	35 A3
Windsor Ct	35 C2
Woodhall Clo	35 D3
Woodlands Rise	35 B3
Woodside Rd	35 B2
Wrenbert Rd	35 B5
York Rd	35 C5

MICKLETON

Alveston Grange	36 A2
Arbour Clo	36 A2
Back La	36 A2
Bakers Hill	36 A3
Ballards Clo	36 A2
Bearcroft Gdns	36 A1
Broad Marston Rd	36 A1
Broadway Rd	36 A3
Campden Rd	36 B1
Cedar Rd	36 B2
Chapel La	36 A2
Cotswold Edge	36 A2
Garden Clo	36 A2
Gloucester La	36 A2
Granbrook La	36 B1
Greyrick Ct	36 B2
High St	36 A1
Inverlea Ct	36 A1
Meon Rd	36 B1
Mill La	36 A2
Norton View	36 B1
Old Manor Gdns	36 B1
Orchard Clo	36 B1
Pound La	36 B1
Stratford Rd	36 B1
Wheatfield Ct	36 A1

MITCHELDEAN

Abenhall Rd	36 B6
Ash Gro	36 B4
Barton Hill	36 B5
Baynham Rd	36 B5
Bradley Ct Rd	36 C4
Brook St	36 C5
Carisbrook Rd	36 D4
Churchill Way	36 B5
Colchester Clo	36 B6
Court Farm La	36 C5
Dean Meadows	36 C5
Deansway	36 D4
Deansway Rd	36 D4
Eastern Av	36 C5
Glebe Clo	36 B4
Gloucester Rd	36 C6
Hawker Hill	36 C5
High St	36 C5
Holywell Rd	36 B4
INDUSTRIAL ESTATES:	
Ladygrove Business Pk	36 D6
Rank Xerox Business Pk	36 C4
May Meadow La	36 B5
New Rd	36 B6
New St	36 B5
Nourse Pl	36 B6
Oakhill Rd	36 C4
Old Dean Rd	36 B4
Orchard Clo	36 B5
Parks Rd	36 C5
Platts Row	36 C5
Ross Rd	36 B4
St Michaels Clo	36 B5
Silver St	36 B6
Stars Pitch	36 C5
Stenders Rd	36 C5
Talbot Pl	36 C5
The Bullring	36 B5
The Crescent	36 B4
The Stenders	36 A6
Townsend	36 B5
Tusculum Way	36 B5
Walwyn Clo	36 B6
Wintles Clo	36 B6

MORETON-IN-MARSH

Bourton Rd	37 A2
Bowes Lyon Ct	37 A3
Bowling Green	37 A1
Corders La	37 A2
Cotsmore Clo	37 C2
Croft Holm	37 B2
Davies Rd	37 C2
Dulverton Pl	37 B2
East St	37 A2
Errington	37 C2
Evenlode Gdns	37 C3
Evenlode Rd	37 C2
Fosseway Av	37 A3
Fosseway Clo	37 B3
Fosseway Dri	37 A3
Grays La	37 B2
High St	37 A2
Hospital Rd	37 A2
Jamieson Ct	37 A3
Keble Rd	37 B3
London Rd	37 B2
*Mead Clo, St Georges Clo	37 B2
Mosedale	37 C1
New Rd	37 B2
Oriel Gro	37 B3
Oxford St	37 A2
Parkers La	37 A2
Primrose Ct	37 A2
Ralph Ct	37 B3
Redesdale Pl	37 B2
St Davids Ct	37 B2
St Davids Walk	37 B2
St Edwards Ct	37 A3
St Georges Clo	37 A3
St James Ct	37 A3
St Pauls Ct	37 A3
St Peters Ct	37 A3
Sawkey Gro	37 B3
Station Rd	37 B2
Stockwells	37 B2
Stow Rd	37 A3
Swan Clo	37 A2
Tinkers Clo	37 B3
The Green	37 B2
Warneford Pl	37 B2
Wellington Rd	37 C2

NAILSWORTH/MINCHINHAMPTON

Avening Rd	38 C5
Badgers Way	38 A4
Barn Clo	38 B5
Barnfield Av	38 A4
Barnfield Rd	38 A4
Bath Rd, Inchbrook	38 A1
Bath Rd, Nailsworth	38 A3
Bell La	39 G2
Besbury La	39 F1
Besbury Park	39 H1
Blue Boys Park	39 G2
Box Cres	39 F3
Box La	38 D3
Brewery La	38 C5
Bridge St	38 C4
Brimscombe Hill	39 E1
Bunting Hill	38 A5
Bunting Way	38 A4
Burfords Grnd	38 A3
Burleigh La	39 E1
Burleigh Tor	39 F1
Burma Rd	38 A4
*Butcher Mills La, Market St	38 C5
Butt St	39 G3
Cambridge Way	39 F2
Carters Way	38 A4
Cecil Ct	39 G2
Chapel Hill	38 C1
Chapel La	39 G3
Cherrytree Clo	38 A4
Chestnut Clo	38 B5
Chestnut Hill	38 B5
Church La	38 C2
Church Rd	38 A3
Church St	38 C5
Churchill Clo	38 B5
Churchill Rd	38 B4
Cirencester Rd	39 E2
Colliers Wood	38 A1
Convent La	38 A1
Cow La	38 C5
Cuckoo Row	39 F3
Culver Hill	38 B1
Dark La	38 B5
Deans Quarry	39 F1
Dr Browns Clo	39 F2
Dr Browns Rd	39 F2
Dr Crawfords Clo	39 F3
Dunkirk Pitch	38 B3
Eastfield Rd	39 H2
Everest Clo	39 E2
Fairview Clo	38 C4
Fewster Rd	38 B5
Fewster Sq	38 B5
Fieldways	38 A4
Firs Rd	38 C5
Fountain St	38 C5
Foxes Dell	38 A4
Friday St	39 G3
Frogmarsh La	38 A1
*Frying Pan Alley, Fewster Rd	38 B5
George St	38 C5
Glebe Rd	39 H2
Grange Clo	38 C5
Gunbarrel Alley	38 C5
Gydynap La	38 B2
Hanover Gdns	38 C5
Hawthorn Ridge	38 A3
Hayes Rd	38 B4
Hiatt Rd	39 F2
High St	39 G3
Higher Newmarket Rd	38 A5
Highcroft	39 F2
Homefield	38 A5
Horsley Rd	38 B6
Inchbrook Hill	38 A3
INDUSTRIAL ESTATES:	
Inchbrook Trading Est	38 B2
Merretts Mill Ind Centre	38 B1
Nailsworth Trading Est	38 D5
Springmill Ind Est	38 E5
Jubilee Rd	38 B4
Kings St	39 G3
Lawnside	38 A4
Love La	39 F1
Lower Newmarket Rd	38 A5
Manor Clo	39 F2
Market Sq	39 G3
Market St	38 C5
Marling Clo	38 C1
Middle Tynings	38 B4
Moffat Rd	38 B4
New Rd	39 F3
Newmarket Rd	38 A5
Northfields Rd	38 A3
Norton Ridge	38 A3
Nortonwood	38 A4
Nympsfield Rd	38 A4
Old Bristol Rd	38 B6
Old Common	39 H2
Old Market	39 F2
Ollney Rd	39 F2
Orchard Mead	38 A2
Park La	38 A2
Park Rd	38 C5
Park Rd Cres	38 C5
Park Ter	39 F3
Parsons Ct	39 G3
Pensile Rd	38 C5
Pike La	38 B5
Plumbers La	38 A5
Ragnal La	38 A6
Ricardo Rd	39 F2
Ringfield Clo	38 B5
Rowan Way	38 A3
St Chloe La	38 B5
St Chloe Mead	38 B1
St Chloes Grn	38 B1
St Marys Hill	38 A2
Scar Hill	38 D4
School Rd	39 G2
Sevenacres Rd	38 A5
Shears Pitch	38 C4
Sheppard Way	39 F2
Shortwood Rd	38 A5
Simmonds Ct	39 G3
Snakes La	38 B3
Southfield	39 F3
Spring Hill	38 B5
Springhill Clo	38 C5
Springhill Cres	38 C5
Star Hill	38 A4
Station Rd	38 C4
Stroud Rd	38 B3
Summersfield Clo	39 H2
Summersfield Rd	39 H2
Syon Rd	39 H2
Tabrams Pitch	38 C5
Tetbury La	38 C6
Tetbury St	39 G3
The Glebe	39 G2
The Knapp	39 G2
The Ladder	38 C4
The Pen	39 E4
The Ridings	38 C6
The Rollers	38 B5
The Roundabouts	39 F1
The Tynings	39 H2
Theescombe Hill	38 B2
Theescombe La	38 B1
Tobacconist Rd	39 G3
Tooke Rd	39 E2
Trinity Dri	39 H2
Tynings Rd	38 B4
Upper Hayes Rd	38 B4
Upper Park Rd	38 C5
Upper Tynings	38 B4
Watledge Bank	38 C4
Watledge Rd	38 B2
Well Hill	39 F3
West End	39 F3
West Tynings	38 B5
Wheelwrights Cnr	38 C5
Whips La	38 B3
Whitecroft	38 B4
Windmill Rd	39 E2
Windsoredge La	38 A3
Woefuldane Bottom	39 H3
Wood La	38 C5
Woodpecker Walk	38 A4
Worley Ridge	38 B5

NEWENT

Akermans Orchard	37 B6
Ash Tree Clo	37 C6
Ayland Clo	37 D5

Bradfords Clo 37 A6
Bradfords La 37 A6
Bridge St 37 B4
Broad St 37 B5
Brookside 37 B6
Bury Bar La 37 C5
Chedworth 37 C5
Church St 37 C5
Church Way 37 C5
Cleeve Rise 37 C5
Coopers Way 37 D6
Court La 37 C5
Court Rd 37 C5
Craddock Rd 37 B6
Croft Clo 37 D5
Croft Rd 37 D5
Culver St 37 B6
Foley Rd 37 C6
Friars Walk 37 B5
Furnace La 37 B4
Gardeners Way 37 B5
Glebe Clo 37 B5
Glebe Ct 37 B5
Glebe Rd 37 A5
Glebe Way 37 B5
Gloucester St 37 C5
Graces Pitch 37 C5
Greenways 37 B5
Hartland 37 D5
High St 37 B5
Hills View 37 C5
Holts Rd 37 B5
Horsefair La 37 A4
INDUSTRIAL ESTATES:
Town Farm Ind Est 37 D5
Johnstone Rd 37 B6
Knights Cres 37 A6
Knights Way 37 A6
Lakeside 37 B5
Market Sq 37 C5
Newlands Ct 37 D5
Old Maids Walk 37 B5
Old Station Rd 37 B4
Onslow Rd 37 C6
Peacock Gdns 37 B6
Perry Clo 37 C5
Pippin Clo 37 C6
Redmarley La 37 C4
Reevers Rd 37 C6
Robinson Clo 37 B5
Ross Rd 37 A5
Rosset Way 37 C6
St Bartholomews 37 C5
Sheppard Way 37 D5
Tewkesbury Rd 37 B4
The Butts 37 C5
The Crease 37 C5
The Crofts 37 C5
The Tythings 37 A6
Tythings Mews 37 B6
Vauxhall 37 A5
Watery La 37 A6
West View 37 A5
Whittington Walk 37 C5
Winfield 37 B6

PAINSWICK

Ashwell 40 C2
Berry Clo 40 C2
Bisley St 40 D2
Blakewell Mead 40 C2
Butt Green 40 C1
Canton Acre 40 D1
Castle Clo 40 C3
Cheltenham Rd 40 D2
Churchill Way 40 C2
Cotswold Mead 40 C3
Court Orchard 40 C3
Edge La 40 A2
Edge Rd 40 B2
Friday St 40 D2
Gloucester Rd 40 D1
Golf Course Rd 40 D1
Greenhouse La 40 D3
Gyde Rd 40 D1
Hale La 40 D3
Hambutts Dri 40 C2
Hollyhock La 40 D2
Hyett Clo 40 C2
Hyett Orchard 40 D2
Kemps La 40 D3
Kingsmead 40 C2
Kingsmill La 40 C3
Knap Las 40 D3
Lower Washwell La 40 D2
New St 40 C2
Orchard Mead 40 D3
Pullens Rd 40 D1
Queens Mead 40 C3
Randalls Field 40 D3
St Marys St 40 D2
Stamages La 40 C3
Stroud Rd 40 B3
*The Churns,
Hale La 40 D3
The Croft 40 C2
The Highlands 40 D1
Tibbiwell 40 D2
Tibbiwell La 40 D2
Upper Washwell 40 D1
Vicarage St 40 D2
Victoria St 40 D2
Whitehorse La 40 D2
Woodborough Clo 40 D3

ST. BRIAVELS

Barrowell La 41 C2
Bream Rd 41 D2
Castle Cres 41 C2
Cinder Hill 41 B2
Cross Keys 41 D2
Crown La 41 C2
East St 41 C1
Hewelsfield La 41 C2
High St 41 C2
Lower Rd 41 B3
Mork Rd 41 C1
Park Clo 41 C2
Pystol La 41 C2
St Annes Way 41 C2
St Bruels Clo 41 C2
Sandy La 41 B3
Smithville Clo 41 D2
Smithville Pl 41 D1
The Square 41 C1
Townsend Clo 41 D2

SEDBURY

*Albion Sq,
Thomas St 42 C3
Arlington Ct 42 E3
Bank St 42 C3
Beachley Rd 42 D1
*Beauford Sq,
High St 42 C3
Beech Gro 42 B4
Bigstone Clo 42 D1
Bigstone Gro 42 D1
Bridge St 42 C2
Bridget Dri 42 E4
Bulwark Rd 42 B3
Buttington Rd 42 E3
Buttington Ter 42 F4
Caird St 42 C3
Castle Gdns 42 B2
Castle View 42 D2
Castleford Gdns 42 C1
Castleford Hill 42 C1
Church Rd 42 C2
Church Row 42 C2
Cliff View 42 E4
Coleford Rd 42 D1
Danes Clo 42 B3
*Davis Ct,
Bridge St 42 C2
Deans Gdns 42 A2
Deans Hill 42 B3
Dell View 42 C3
Denmark Dri 42 E4
Edmond Rd 42 E2
Elm Clo 42 E1
Elm Rd 42 D1
Elmdale 42 C2
Exmouth Pl 42 C3
Fair View 42 B4
Fairfield Rd 42 C4
Fitzosborne Clo 42 33
Garden City Way 42 C3
Gloucester Rd 42 D1
Grahamstown Gro 42 E2
Grahamstown Rd 42 E3
Green St 42 C3
Gwentlands Clo 42 B4
Gwy Ct 42 C2
Hanover Clo 42 A2
Hanover Ct 42 E3
Hardwick Av 42 C3
Hardwick Hill 42 B3
Hardwick Hill La 42 B3
Hardwick Ter 42 B3
Hendrick Dri 42 E3
High Beech La 42 A4
High St 42 C3
High View 42 B3
Hilltop 42 B4
Hocker Hill St 42 C2
Hollins Clo 42 C2
Howells Row 42 D2
Hughes Cres 42 C4
Huntfield Rd 42 A2
Kendall Sq 42 D2
King Alfreds Rd 42 E4
Kingsmark La 42 A2
Lancaster Way 42 B2
Larkfield Av 42 B4
Larkhill Clo 42 B4
*Library Pl,
Bank St 42 C3
Lower Church St 42 C2
Madocke Rd 42 E3
*Manor Way,
Bank St 42 C3
Marten Rd 42 C4
Mathern Rd 42 B4
Meadow Wk 42 B3
Mercian Way 42 E4
Middle St 42 C2
Mill La 42 C3
*Montague Almshouse,
Upper Church St 42 C2
Moor St 42 C3
Mopla Rd 42 C1
Mount Pleasant 42 B3
Mount Way 42 B2
Mounton Clo 42 B3
Mounton Dri 42 B3
Mounton Rd 42 A3
Myrtle Pl 42 D2
Nelson St 42 C3
Newport Rd 42 B4
Normandy Way 42 A2
Norse Way 42 E3
Oakfield Av 42 A2
Offas Clo 42 E4
Old Bulwark Rd 42 B4
Orchard Clo 42 C2
Orchard Farm Clo 42 E4
Ormerod Rd 42 E3
Park View,
Chepstow 42 A2
Park View,
Sedbury 42 F3
Penda Pl 42 E3
Piercefield Av 42 A2
Port Wall 42 C3
Portwall Rd 42 C3
Priory Clo 42 B2
Regent Way 42 B3
Restway Wall 42 C3
*Riflemans Way,
Bank St 42 C3
River Vw 42 C3
Rockwood Rd 42 C3
Ruffetts Clo 42 B3
St Andrews Av 42 C4
St Anns St 42 C2
St Davids Clo 42 C4
St Georges Rd 42 C4
St Johns Gdns 42 A2
St Kingsmark Av 42 B2
St Lawrence La 42 A4
St Lawrence Rd 42 A2
St Marys St 42 C2
St Maur Gdns 42 B2
St Tecla Rd 42 C4
St Tewdric Rd 42 B4
Saxon Pl 42 E3
School La 42 C3
Sedbury La 42 E2
Severn Av 42 D2
Severn Cres 42 C4
Silleys Clo 42 D1
Station Rd 42 C3
Steep St 42 B3
Strongbow Rd 42 C4
Stuart Clo 42 B2
Tallards Pl 42 E3
The Back 42 D2
The Martins 42 E2
The Myrtles 42 E1
The Old Hill 42 C1
The Paddock 42 B4
The Priory 42 C2
The Yetts 42 E3
*Thomas Powis
Almshouses,
Bridge St 42 C2
Thomas St 42 C3
Tudor Dri 42 A2
Turnike Clo 42 A2
Tuts Hill Gdns 42 D2
Tylers Way 42 E3
Upper Church St 42 C2
Upper Nelson St 42 C3
Vauxhall La 42 B3
Vauxhall Rd 42 B3
Warwick Clo 42 B4
Waters Rd 42 C3
Welsh St 42 A1
Wintour Clo 42 A2
Wirewood Clo 42 D1
Wirewood Cres 42 D1
Wye Cres 42 C4
Wye Valley Link Rd 42 B4
Wyebank Av 42 D2
Wyebank Clo 42 D3
Wyebank Cres 42 D3
Wyebank Pl 42 D3
Wyebank Rise 42 E3
Wyebank Road 42 D3
Wyebank View 42 E3
Wyebank Way 42 D3

SHURDINGTON

Atherton Clo 43 B2
Badgeworth La 43 A2
Bishop Rd 43 B2
Blenheim Orchard 43 C1
Church La 43 B2
Cowls Mead 43 B2
Farm La 43 B3
Greenway Clo 43 B3
Greenway La 43 B3
Gwinnett Ct 43 C2
Harrison Rd 43 B2
Lambert Av 43 A3
Lambert Clo 43 B2
Lambert Dri 43 B2
Lambert Gdns 43 B3
Lambert Ter 43 B2
Laurence Clo 43 B2
Lawn Cres 43 C2
Leckhampton La 43 C2
Marsh Ter 43 B2
Robertson Rd 43 B2
School La 43 C2
Shurdington Rd 43 B3
Sinclair Rd 43 B2
The Orchard Gro 43 B3
Vicarage Clo 43 C2
Wilson Rd 43 B2
Yarnolds 43 B2

SOUTH CERNEY

Beaverstone Clo 41 B6
Beaverstone Rd 41 B6
Berkeley Clo 41 B6
Bow Wow 41 C5
Boxbush Clo 41 C5
Boxbush Rd 41 C5
Broadway La 41 B6
Church La 41 B5
Churn Clo 41 B5
Clarks Way 41 B5
Edwards College 41 B4
Field Clo 41 C5
Ham La 41 C6
High St 41 B6
Huxley Ct 41 C5
Jubilee Gdns 41 B5
Kingfisher Pl 41 C5
Lakeside 41 D5
Langet 41 B5
Meadow Way 41 B5
Mill Clo 41 C5
Oak Way 41 C6
Paymans Ter 41 B5
River Way 41 B5
Robert Franklin Way 41 D5
School La 41 B5
Silver St 41 B4
Station Rd 41 C5
Sudeley Dri 41 B6
The Close 41 C5
The Leaze 41 B6
The Lennards 41 C5
The Paddock 41 B5
Timbrells Clo 41 B5
Wildmoorway La 41 D5
Willow Gro 41 C5

STONEHOUSE

Abbots Clo 46 C6
Adelaide Gdns 46 C3
Albany 46 C3
Aldergate St 46 D5
Anderson Dri 46 D5
Avenue Ter 46 B5
Barlow Clo 46 B5
Bath Rd 46 C5
Blackbird Ct 46 D4
Boakes Dri 46 B5
Bramble La 46 D4
Bridgend Ct 46 C6
Brisbane 46 C3
Bristol Rd 46 A4
Browns La 46 D6
Brunel Way 46 A4
Burdett 46 D5
Burdett Clo 46 D5
Canberra 46 C3
Cedar Gdns 46 D4
Chaffinch Clo 46 D4
Chapel Row 46 C5
Chestnut Av 46 C4
Church La 46 B5
Coates Gdns 46 D4
College View 46 D5
Cotswold Grn 46 D4
Crescent Clo 46 C6
Crescent Rd 46 C6
Crest Ct 46 D4
Downton Rd 46 C6
Ebley By-Pass 46 D6
Ebley Rd 46 D6
Elms Rd 46 C4
Festival Rd 46 B5
Glen Ct 46 D4
Glenthorne Clo 46 D3
Gloucester Rd 46 C4
Green St 46 C4
Grosvenor Rd 46 C3
Haven Av 46 C6
High St 46 C4
INDUSTRIAL ESTATES:
Bonds Mill Ind Est 46 A5
Button Mill Ind Est 46 B6
Oldends Lane
Ind Est 46 B4
Stonehouse Comm.
Centre 46 B5
Stroudwater
Business Park 46 A4
Upper Mills Ind Est 46 C6
Juniper Way 46 D4
Kestrel Ct 46 D4
Kimmins Rd 46 D4
Kings Rd 46 C3
Laburnum Mews 46 C5
Laburnum Rd 46 C5
Laburnum Walk 46 C5
Magpie Ct 46 D4
Meadow Rd 46 C4
Meadway Rd 46 C6
Melbourne Clo 46 C3
Melbourne Dri 46 C3
Midland Rd 46 B4
Nasted La 46 C3
Nursery Ter 46 C6
Oak Way 46 D5
Oldends La 46 A5
Orchard Ct 46 C5
Orchard Pl 46 C5
Osprey Dri 46 D4
Paddock Rise 46 D4
Park Par 46 C4
Park Rd 46 B5
Partridge Clo 46 D4
Pearcroft Rd 46 D6
Perth 46 C3
Pheasant Mead 46 D4
Queens Rd 46 C5
Quietways 46 C4
Regent St 46 C5
Robin Ct 46 D4
Rosedale Av 46 D5
Ryelands Clo 46 C4
Ryelands Rd 46 C4
St Cyrils Rd 46 D5
Severn Rd 46 B4
Sherborne Ct 46 D4
Starling Ct 46 D4
Stonedale Rd 46 B4

Storrington Pl 46 D5
Storrington Rd 46 D5
Sydney 46 C3
The Lawns 46 C4
The Square 46 C4
Upper Queens Rd 46 D5
Verney Rd 46 D5
Wharfedale Way 46 C6
Whitefield 46 C6
Willow Rd 46 B5
Woodcock Clo 46 D4
Woodcock La 46 C4

STOW-ON-THE-WOLD

Back Walls 43 B5
Bailey Clo 43 C5
Bartletts Park 43 B6
Camp Gdns 43 B5
Chamberlay Clo 43 B6
Chapel St 43 B5
Church St 43 B5
Clifton Clo 43 B5
Digbeth St 43 B5
Evesham Rd 43 A4
Fisher Clo 43 B6
Fosse Folly 43 B4
Fosse La 43 B4
Fosseway 43 B5
Glebe Clo 43 B5
Griffin Clo 43 D5
High St 43 B5
Jubilee Clo 43 B5
King Georges Field 43 C5
Lower Park St 43 B5
Market Sq 43 B5
Maugersbury Park 43 B6
Mount Pleasant Clo 43 C5
Oddington Rd 43 C5
Park St 43 B5
St Edwards Dri 43 C5
St Edwards Rd 43 C5
Sheep St 43 B5
Shepherds Row 43 B5
Shepherds Way 43 B5
Station Rd 43 B1
Talbot Cotts 43 B5
Talbot Ct 43 B5
Talbot Sq 43 B5
The Courtyard 43 B4
The Park 43 B6
The Stables 43 B5
Union St 43 B5
Well La 43 B4

STROUD

Acre St 45 E5
All Saints Rd 45 E4
Allen Dri 44 B4
Archway Gdns 44 B4
Arundel Dri 44 D6
Arundel Mill La 45 E6
Barrowfield Rd 44 B3
Bath Rd 44 B6
Bath St 44 D5
Beards La 44 B5
Bedford St 44 D5
Beeches Grn 44 D4
Belle Vue Clo 45 E5
Belle Vue Rd 45 E5
Belmont Rd 45 F6
Birches Clo 45 E4
Birches Dri 44 D4
Bisley Old Rd 45 E5
Bisley Rd 45 E5
Bowbridge La 45 E6
Brewery Rd 44 A5
Briar Clo 45 E3
Brick Row 45 E5
Bridge Side 44 A6
Bridge St 44 A6
Burford Dri 44 C5
Byron Rd 44 B4
Cainscross Rd 44 A5
Capel Ct 45 E4
Captain Barton Clo 45 F4
Cashes Green Rd 44 A5
Castle Pitch 45 E6
Castle Rise 45 E6
Castle St 45 E6
Castlemead Rd 44 C6
Catherines Clo 45 F5
Central Rd 44 B5
Chapel St 45 E5
Cheapside 44 D5
Chestnut La 44 B5
Church St 44 D5
Churchfield Rd 45 F6
Clare Ct 45 F5
College Rd 44 B4
Cornhill 44 D5
Coronation Rd 44 A4
Cotswold Rd 44 A4
Cotteswold Rise 45 E5
Cowle Rd 45 E6
Cutler Rd 45 E4
Daisy Bank 45 F6
Daniels Rd 45 G5
Delmont Gro 44 D4
Dr Newtons Way 44 D5
Downfield 44 B4
Downfield Rd 44 B5
Dudbridge Rd 44 A6
Dudbridge Hill 44 B6
Duderstadt Clo 44 B4
Elm Rd 44 A4
Far Leazes 45 E5
Farmhill Cres 44 B3
Farmhill La 44 B4
Farrs La 44 D5
*Fawkes Pl,
    Bedford St 44 D5
Ferndale Rd 44 B1
Field Rd, Stroud 44 C6
Field Rd,
    Whiteshill 44 B1
Folly La 44 D4
Folly Rise 45 E3
Fort View Ter 44 A6
Frome Av 44 C6
Frome Gdns 44 A6
Frome Hall La 44 C6
Frome Park Av 44 B6
Fromeside 44 D6
Gannicox Rd 44 C5
George St 44 D5
Gibson Clo 45 G5
Gloucester St 44 D5
Grange View 45 E4
Grove Park Rd 45 E4
Heathfield Rd 44 B3
Heazle Pl 44 D4
High St 44 D5
Highfield Rd,
    Stroud 45 F6
Highfield Rd,
    Whiteshill 44 B1
Hill Top Clo 45 G5
Hillfield 44 B5
Hillier Clo 45 F3
Hollow La 45 E5
Horns Rd 45 E6
Humphreys Clo 44 A4
Hyett Rd 44 A5
INDUSTRIAL ESTATES:
Lightpill Trading Est 44 C6
Salmon Springs
    Depot 44 D3
John Bevan 45 E4
John St 44 D5
Keats Gdns 44 B3
Kendrick St 44 D5
Kilminster Rd 45 G5
King St 44 D5
Kingley Rd 44 A5
Kings Rd 44 A5
Knapp La 45 H2
Langtoft 45 F5
Lansdown 44 D5
Leazes Pitch 45 E5
Libbys Dri 45 E4
Lightwood La 44 A1
Locking Hill 44 D5
Lodgemore Clo 44 C5
Lodgemore La 44 B5
London Field La 45 E5
London Rd 44 D4
Lovedays Mead 44 D4
Lower Churchfield Rd 45 F6
Lower Kitesnest La 44 B1
Lower Leazes 45 E5
Lower Spillmans 45 E6
Lower St, Stroud 45 E6
Lower St,
    Whiteshill 44 B1
Main Rd 44 B1
Maldon Ter 44 D5
Maple Dri 44 B5
Marling Cres 44 A4
Mason Rd 45 G5
Mathews Way 44 B4
Meadow La West 44 A6
Merrywalks 44 D5
Middle Hill 45 F5
Middle Leazes 45 E5
Middle Spillmans 44 C6
Middle St,
    Stroud Hill 45 E5
Middle St, Uplands 45 E4
Mill Farm Dri 44 A4
Milton Gro 44 F5
Moor Hall Pl 44 A4
Mosley Cres 44 A5
Mosley Rd 44 A4
Nelson St 45 E5
Northfield Mews 45 E4
Nouncells Cross 45 F5
Nursery Clo 45 E6
Oak Dri 44 C6
Paganhill Est 44 A4
Paganhill La 44 A5
Painswick Old Rd 44 D4
Painswick Rd 44 C3
Park End Rd 44 A3
Park Rd 45 E6
Park View Dri 44 A4
Parliament Clo 45 E5
Parliament St 45 E5
Paynes Pl 44 B6
Peghouse Clo 45 F3
Peghouse Rise 45 E3
Queens Dri 44 A4
Queens Rd 44 C6
Reservoir Clo 45 G5
Reservoir Rd 45 F6
Ridgemont Rd 45 F6
Rodborough Av 44 C6
Rodborough Hill 44 C6
Row Croft 44 D5
Rowcroft Retreat 44 D5
Russell St 44 D5
*Rye Lease Clo,
    Rye Lease Rd 45 E5
Rye Lease Rd 45 D5
St Brendans Rd 45 F5
Selsley Hill 44 A6
Shepherds Clo 45 E4
Shepherds Croft 45 E4
Shooters End 44 D4
Slad La 45 G4
Slad Rd 44 D5
Slade Brook 45 F4
Spider La 45 F6
Spillmans Rd 44 C6
Spring La 44 C6
Springfield Rd 44 A4
Stanton Rd 44 A4
Station Rd 44 D5
Strachans Clo 44 B5
Stratford Rd 44 B4
Streamside 45 E5
Summer Clo 45 F5
Summer Cres 45 F5
Summer St 45 E5
Sutton Pl 45 E5
Swifts Hill View 45 F3
Sycamore Dri 45 E4
Target Clo 45 G5
The Budding 45 F3
The Circle 45 E4
The Hill 44 C5
The Plain 44 B2
The Shambles 44 D5
The Square 45 E4
The Woodlands 45 E4
Thompson Rd 45 E4
Threadneedle St 44 D5
Trinity Rd 45 E6
Union St 44 D5
Uplands Rd 45 E4
Upper Kitesnest La 44 B1
Upper Leazes 45 E5
Upper Springfield Rd 45 E4
Valley View Rd 45 G6
Victory Rd 44 B1
Wades La 44 D1
Wall Bridge 44 D5
Well End 45 F4
Wesley Ct 45 E5
West Ct Grange 44 D4
Westward Rd 44 A6
Wheelers Walk 44 B4
White Hall 45 E5
Whitehouse Park 44 A5
Wickridge Clo 45 E4
Woodhouse Dri 44 D6
Woodlands Dri 45 F4

TETBURY

Alexander Gdns 47 D2
Bartley Croft 47 D2
Bath Rd 47 C4
Beech Tree Gdns 47 D2
Berkley Way 47 D1
Berrells Rd 47 C4
Black Horse Hill 47 C3
Blind La 47 D1
Chantry Ct 47 D3
Charlton Rd 47 B3
Chavenage La 47 B1
Cherry Orchard Dri 47 D2
Chestnut Clo 47 C2
Cheviot Clo 47 D1
Chipping Steps 47 D3
Chipping St 47 D3
Church St 47 D3
Cirencester Rd 47 D3
Clarrie Rd 47 D1
Close Gdns 47 C3
Combers End 47 D2
Conygar Rd 47 D1
Cook Spool 47 D2
Coronation Rd 47 C1
Cotswold Clo 47 D1
Cottons La 47 C3
Court Field 47 C2
Cutwell 47 C3
Eccles Ct 47 D3
Elizabeth Gdns 47 C2
Five Trees Ct 47 C2
Fox Hill 47 D3
Gastrall Ct 47 D2
Grange La 47 C4
Grove Gdns 47 C1
Gumstool Hill 47 D3
Hampton St 47 C1
Herd La 47 E3
Highfield Rd 47 C1
Hodges Clo 47 D2
Hookhouse La 47 A4
INDUSTRIAL ESTATES:
Hampton St Ind Est 47 B1
Priory Ind Est 47 D2
Tetbury Ind Est 47 E2
The Old Quarry
    Ind Units 47 D4
Jacobs Clo 47 D1
Linfoot Rd 47 C3
London Rd 47 D2
Long St 47 C3
Longfurlong La 47 B4
Longtree Clo 47 C1
Love La 47 D3
Lowfield Rd 47 C1
Magdalen Rd 47 C2
Malthouse Walk 47 D2
Market Pl 47 D3
New Church St 47 C3
New Leaze Gdns 47 C2
Newnton Rd 47 D3
Northfield Clo 47 E2
Northfield Rd 47 D2
Northlands Way 47 D1
Northleaze 47 E2
Old Brewery La 47 D3
Oxleaze Clo 47 C2
Oxleaze Rd 47 C2
Park Clo 47 D2
Priory Way 47 D2
Quail Meadows 47 C2
Romney Rd 47 C1
Ryland Clo 47 D1
St Marys Rd 47 C2
Shepherds Mead 47 D1
Sherwood Rd 47 C3
Silver St 47 C4
Southfield 47 C4
Springfields 47 E2
Starveal La 47 C4
Suffolk Clo 47 D1
Talbots Walk 47 C4
The Berrells 47 C4
The Chipping 47 D3
The Damsels 47 D2
The Ferns 47 D3
The Green 47 D3
Upton Gdns 47 C1
Wains Ct 47 D3
West St 47 C2
Wheat Hill 47 D2
Windsor Gdns 47 C2
Wistaria Rd 47 C2
Woodward Clo 47 C1

TEWKESBURY

Abbots Rd 48 B6
Abbots Walk 48 A6
Alexandra Way 49 G3
Alpha Clo 49 E3
Arundel Rd 48 C2
Ash Rd 49 G2
Ashchurch Rd 48 C4
Avon View 48 D2
Back of Avon 48 B4
Barton Ct 48 C4
Barton Mews 48 B4
Barton Rd 48 B4
Barton St 48 B4
Battle Rd 48 A6
Beaufort Pl 48 B6
Beta Clo 49 F2
Bevan Gdns 49 H1
Bishops Walk 48 B3
Bowler Rd 49 H1
Bramley Rd 48 C3
Bredon Rd 48 B3
Brensham Rd 49 E3
Brookside 48 D2
Canterbury Leys 48 D3
Carrant Rd 48 C3
Cedar Rd 49 G2
Chance St 48 B4
Cherry Orchard 49 H2
Church St 48 A4
Churchill Gro 48 D4
Clarence Rd 48 B6
*Collins Ct,
    Back of Avon 48 B4
*Comptons Alley,
    Barton St 48 B4
Conigree La 48 B6
Cotswold Gdns 48 C3
Cotteswold Rd 48 B3
Coventry Clo 48 B6
Cromers Clo 49 G1
Curlew Clo 49 G1
Delta Rd 49 E3
Derwent Dri 48 D2
Despenser Rd 48 B5
Devonshire Pl 48 B6
Digby Dri 48 C2
East St 48 B4
Elm Rd 49 H2
Elmbury Dri 49 E3
Elmvil Rd 49 E3
Fairway 49 G2
Farm Clo 49 G2
*Fletchers Alley,
    Barton St 48 B4
Folly Gdns 48 B4
Foresters Pl 48 B5
Gander La 48 A4
Gannaway La 49 E3
George Dowty Dri 49 G1
Gloucester Rd 48 A5
Gould Dri 49 G1
Grange Ct 49 H2
Grange Rd 49 H1
Gravel Walk 48 B3
Green La 49 E3
Greystone Clo 48 D2
Gupshill Clo 48 B6
*Hanover Ct,
    Back of Avon 48 B4
Harbourside 48 B2
Hardwick Bank Rd 49 G1
Hastings Pl 48 B6
Hawthorn Way 49 H1
High St 48 B4
Hollams Rd 48 B3
Hone Ct 48 B4
Howard Clo 49 G2
Howard Rd 49 G2
Howells Rd 48 B4
INDUSTRIAL ESTATES:
Ashchurch Ind Est 49 F3
Northway Trading
    Est 49 H3
Tewkesbury
    Business Centre 49 F3
Tewkesbury
    Ind Est 49 E3
Jeynes Row 48 B3
Kestrel Way 49 G1

King Johns Ct 48 B3
Kings Gate 49 E3
Kingston Rd 49 G2
Knights Way 48 D4
Lancaster Rd 48 B6
Lanes Ct 48 B4
Lapwing Clo 49 G1
Lee Rd 49 H2
*Lilleys Alley,
  Barton St 48 B4
Lincoln Clo 48 A6
Lincoln Green La 48 A6
Link Rd 48 B4
Long Eights 49 G2
Lower Lode La 48 A5
Manor Park 48 D2
Manor Pl 48 B6
Margaret Rd 48 B5
Meadow Clo 48 D2
Mill St 48 A4
Milne Pastures 49 E3
Mitton Way 48 C2
Monkey Meadow 49 G1
Moulder Rd 48 D4
Mount Pleasant Rd,
  Barton St 48 B4
Mythe Rd 48 A2
Naylor Ct,
  Back of Avon 48 B4
Nelson St 48 B4
Neville Rd 48 B5
Newtown La 48 D3
Northway La 48 D3
Oak Dri 49 G2
Old Manor La 48 D2
Old Post Office La,
  Oldbury Rd 48 B4
Oldbury Rd 48 B4
Oldfield 48 B4
Orchard Ct 48 B4
Park Clo 49 G1
Priors Alley 48 A4
Priors Ct,
  Back of Avon 48 B4
Ryke Rd 48 D4
Quay St 48 B3
Queens Rd 48 B5
Red La 48 B3
Redwood Ct 49 H2
Richard Pl 48 B6
Robin Clo 49 G1
Ropewalk 48 B4
Rosefield Cres 48 D4
Saffron Rd 48 B4
St Davids Rd 49 H3
St Marys La 48 A4
St Marys Rd 48 A4
Sallis Clo 49 G1
Seymour St 48 B5
Shakespeare Ct,
  Back of Avon 48 B4
Shannon Way 48 E3
Shephard Mead 48 A5
Sunderberry Dri 49 H1
Smiths La 48 B3
Somerset Clo 48 B6
Spa Gdns 48 D4
Springfield 48 D3
Stanford Rd 49 G2
Stanton Rd 48 C2
Station La 48 C3
Station Rd 48 B3
Station St 48 B3
Steward Rd 49 G2
Stokes Ct 48 B4
Sun St 48 B4
Tilvgate Rd 48 B4
Sycamore Rd 49 G2
Twyny Rd 49 F1
Wkesbury Rd 48 D1
The Apple Orchard 49 G1
The Hopyard 49 G1
The Park 49 G1
The Pear Orchard 49 G1
The Sandfield 49 G2
Theocs Clo 48 A6
Thistle Downs 49 G1
The Bank Way 48 D4
Ilsey La 48 B4
Tetawn Gdns 48 D4
Trinity St 48 B4
Boughton Pl 48 D4
Tudor Pl 48 B6
Tug Wilson Clo 49 G1
Vixtbears 48 B3
Virginia Clo 49 H2
Virginia Rd 49 H2
Wagtail Dri 49 G1

Walkley Rd 48 B3
Walls Ct 48 B4
Warren Rd 49 G2
Warwick Pl 48 B5
Watledge Clo 48 B4
Well Clo 49 G2
Wellfield 49 E3
Wenlock Rd 48 B5
Westfield Av 49 G2
Wheatstone Clo 49 G1
Willis Walk 49 G1
Wynyards Clo 48 C4
*Yarnells Alley,
  Barton St 48 B4
York Rd 48 B6

THORNBURY

Alexandra Way 50 B3
Armstrong Clo 50 D6
Ashgrove 50 C5
Avon Way 50 C6
Bath Rd 50 B5
Blakes Rd 50 B5
Bockenem 50 D6
Brookmead 50 C6
Brunel Way 50 B6
Buckingham Par 50 B4
Butts La 50 B2
Castle Coombe 50 B4
Castle Clo 50 B5
Castle St 50 A4
Catsbrain La 50 D1
Celandine Clo 50 D3
Chantry Rd 50 B4
Chapel St 50 B5
Charles Clo 50 C2
Chatsworth Pk 50 C3
Cherwell Clo 50 C6
Chestnut Dri 50 C4
Cheviot Dri 50 D5
Chiltern Vw 50 D6
Church Rd 50 A4
Clare Walk 50 B4
Cleveland Clo 50 D5
Colin Clo 50 B5
Colne Sq 50 C6
Combermere Av 50 C5
Coombe Av 50 B4
Cooper Rd 50 B6
Cossham Clo 50 C3
Crispin La 50 B5
Crossways Rd 50 D4
Cumbria Clo 50 D5
Dean Av 50 B3
Derwent Ct 50 D6
Dovedale 50 D6
Dyrham Clo 50 C2
Eastbury Clo 50 C4
Eastbury Rd 50 C4
Eastland Av 50 C4
Eastland Rd 50 C4
Easton Hill Rd 50 B4
Elizabeth Clo 50 D5
Ellesmere 50 C5
Elmdale Cres 50 C5
Eskdale 50 C6
Falcon Way 50 C4
Finch Clo 50 C3
Foxglove Clo 50 D4
Frome Ct 50 B5
Fulmar Clo 50 C3
Gillingstool 50 B5
Gloucester Rd 50 B4
Grovesend Rd 50 C5
Hacket La 50 D4
Hamble Clo 50 C5
Hatchmere 50 C5
Hawthorne Cres 50 C4
Hazel Cres 50 C4
High St 50 A6
Hillbrook Rd 50 D5
Hillcrest 50 B5
Homefield 50 C5
Hopkin Clo 50 C6
Horse La 50 D1
Howard Rd 50 B3
Hyde Av 50 B3
Jubilee Dri 50 D5
Kempton Clo 50 B2
Kennet Way 50 D5
Kensington Clo 50 B3
Kestrel Clo 50 C4
Kingfisher Clo 50 D3
Kington La 50 A5
Knapp Rd 50 C5

Ladden Ct 50 C6
Larkspur Clo 50 D4
Lavender Clo 50 D4
Mallow Clo 50 D3
Malvern Dri 50 D6
Manor Walk 50 B2
Maple Av 50 C4
Meadowside 50 C5
Medina Ct 50 D6
Medway Ct 50 B5
Midland Rd 50 B5
Midland Way 50 D6
Millfields 50 B3
Millfields Clo 50 B3
Morton St 50 C1
Morton Way 50 C2
Nightingale Clo 50 D3
North East Rd 50 C3
North Rd 50 C4
Oakleaze Rd 50 C5
Oldbury La 50 A1
Orchard Av 50 B3
Orchard Grange 50 A4
Osprey Pk 50 D3
Park Rd 50 B3
Park View Rd 50 C4
Parkland Way 50 B2
Pentland Dri 50 D5
Pine Clo 50 C4
Pittville Clo 50 C2
Primrose Clo 50 D3
Pulling Grn 50 B5
Quaker La 50 B5
Queens Walk 50 B5
Rabley Rd 50 B4
Raglan Pl 50 B5
Regent Clo 50 B3
Ribblesdale 50 C6
Rock St 50 B5
Rosslyn Way 50 B2
St Davids Rd 50 B5
St John St 50 B5
St Marys Rd 50 B5
St Marys Way 50 B5
Sawmill La 50 B5
Severn Dri 50 B4
Severn View Rd 50 C3
Shannon Ct 50 D6
Short Way 50 B6
Sibland 50 D5
Sibland Clo 50 D5
Sibland Rd 50 D5
Sibland Way 50 C5
Solent Way 50 D6
Sorrel Clo 50 D4
Speedwell Clo 50 D3
Spey Clo 50 C5
Springfield 50 C5
Squires Leaze 50 C3
Stafford Cres 50 B4
Stokefield Clo 50 A4
Streamleaze 50 B5
Streamside Walk 50 B3
Swallow Pk 50 C2
Sycamore Dri 50 C4
Tamar Clo 50 D6
The Paddocks 50 C5
The Plain 50 B5
Thicket Walk 50 C4
Tiling Rd 50 B4
Trent Dri 50 D6
Tyndale View 50 B5
Upper Bath Rd 50 B5
Victoria Clo 50 B3
Vilner La 50 B6
Walker Way 50 B6
Walnut Clo 50 C4
Warwick Pl 50 A4
Waterford Clo 50 D6
Wharfedale 50 C6
Whitfield Rd 50 C6
Windrush Ct 50 C6
Woodleigh 50 C5
Wye Clo 50 C6

UPPER LYDBROOK

Camomile Grn 51 B5
Church Hill 51 B3
Church Rd 51 B3
Church View 51 B3
Coppice Rd 51 A2
Eddys La 51 D1
Edwards Clo 51 B2
Forest Rd 51 B4

Forge Hill 51 A1
Greenfield Clo 51 B2
Greenfield Rd 51 B2
Hatton Clo 51 B5
High St 51 D2
Highbeech Rd 51 D2
Hillside Ter 51 B2
Horselea 51 B2
Joys Green Rd 51 B2
New Rd 51 A6
Orchard Rd 51 B2
Probertsbarn La 51 A2
Ridge Pl 51 B6
Rocks Rd 51 A2
School Cres 51 B2
School Rd,
  Joys Green 51 B2
School Rd,
  Upper Lydbrook 51 B4
Squires Rd 51 A4
The Bourts 51 B5
Uphill Rd 51 B2
Valley Rd 51 B6
Vention La 51 B1
Worral Hill 51 B6
Wye View Rd 51 B2

WINCHCOMBE

Abbey Ter 52 B3
Abbots Leys Rd 52 A3
Back La 52 B3
Barksdale 52 A3
Barnmeadow Rd 52 B2
Bassett Clo 52 B1
Bicks La 52 C2
Binyon Rd 52 A3
Blenheim Ct 52 B2
Broadway Rd 52 C2
Brook Clo 52 A3
Bull La 52 C2
Castle St 52 C3
Cedar Gro 52 B1
Chandos St 52 C2
Cheltenham Rd 52 A3
Clarendon Rd 52 B1
Cow La 52 B2
Crispin Clo 52 B1
Crispin Rd 52 B1
Delavale Rd 52 B1
Dents Ter 52 B3
Eldersfield Clo 52 B1
Gervase Rd 52 B1
Gillette Clo 52 B3
Gloucester St 52 B3
Godwin Rd 52 B1
Greenways 52 C1
Greet Rd 52 B1
Gretton Rd 52 B1
Hailes St 52 C2
Harveys La 52 A3
High St 52 C3
Huddleston Rd 52 B1
Kenelm Rise 52 B1
Kenulf Rd 52 C2
Kyderminster Clo 52 B3
Langley Clo 52 B1
Langley Rd 52 A3
Malthouse La 52 B2
Mercia Rd 52 B2
Mill La 52 C2
North St 52 B1
Norton Clo 52 B1
Orchard Rd 52 B2
Puck Pit La 52 D1
Rathmore Clo 52 B1
Riverside 52 C1
Rushley La 52 C2
St Peters Way 52 B2
Seymour Pl 52 B2
Silk Mill La 52 C3
Spittle Leys 52 B2
Stancombe 52 C2
Stancombe La 52 D2
Stancombe View 52 C2
Summers Rd 52 B2
The Hyde 52 A3
Tobacco Clo 52 A3
Vineyard St 52 B3
Whitmore Rd 52 B1
Wincel Rd 52 C1

WINTERBOURNE/FRAMPTON COTTERELL

Abbeydale 53 B3
Alexandra Rd 53 F2

Badminton Rd 53 E4
Barley Clo 53 E1
Barton Clo 53 A4
Beaufort Rd 53 D1
Beaver Clo 53 C2
Beesmoor Rd 53 E2
Bell Rd 53 E3
Boundary Rd 53 F2
Bourne Clo 53 B2
Bradley Av 53 A4
Bradstone Rd 53 A4
Branksome Dri 53 A3
Bridge Way 53 E1
Bristol Rd 53 A2
Brockridge La 53 E2
Brookside Dri 53 D1
Burghley Ct 53 B4
Burrough Way 53 A4
Camberley Dri 53 B1
Cannons 53 A2
Church Clo 53 E1
Church La,
  Frampton Cotterell 53 F3
Church La,
  Winterbourne 53 A3
Church Rd 53 C1
Cloisters Rd 53 B3
Clyde Rd 53 E1
Common Rd 53 B2
Court Rd 53 B1
Crossley Clo 53 B2
Crossman Av 53 A4
Dawley Clo 53 B2
Deacon Clo 53 A4
Dormer Clo 53 F3
Downfield Dri 53 E2
Dragon Rd 53 A4
Englands Cres 53 B2
Factory Rd 53 C2
Fernleaze 53 F3
Flaxpits La 53 A3
Footes La 53 E2
Fox Rd 53 D1
Frampton End Rd 53 F1
Friary Grange Park 53 A3
Frome View 53 D2
Frome Way 53 B4
Gladstone La 53 E2
Gledemoor Dri 53 F2
Goose Grn 53 E1
Green Dragon Rd 53 B3
Green La 53 A2
Harcombe Rd 53 A4
Harris Barton 53 D2
Heath Clo 53 B3
Heath Gdns 53 F4
Heathcote Dri 53 D3
Heather Av 53 D3
Henfield Rd 53 F4
Hicks Common Rd 53 B4
High St 53 A3
Hillside Clo 53 F2
Hillside La 53 E2
Holmwood Clo 53 A3
Huckford Rd 53 A4
Langthorn Clo 53 E2
Larkfield 53 F2
Lewton La 53 B2
Linden Clo 53 A3
Lower Chapel La 53 E3
Lower Stone Clo 53 F1
Ludwell Clo 53 F2
Main View 53 F2
Manor Clo 53 E3
Manor La 53 C2
Masons Clo 53 B3
Matford Clo 53 B4
Meadow Mead 53 D1
Meadow View 53 B2
Medway Dri 53 D3
Mill Clo 53 E3
Mill La,
  Frampton Cotterell 53 E2
Mill La,
  Frampton End 53 D1
Mount Clo 53 C1
Mount Cres 53 A4
Newlands Av 53 F3
Nicholls La 53 A2
Nightingale Clo 53 D3
North Rd 53 B2
Oakleaze 53 F3
Oldlands Av 53 F3
Orchard Clo 53 B4
Orchard Rd 53 F2
Park Av,
  Frampton Cotterell 53 D3

Street	Ref
Park Av, Winterbourne	53 B3
Park La	53 D3
Park Row	53 D1
Parkside Av	53 A3
Pendock Rd	53 B4
Prospect Clo	53 C1
Prospect La	53 C1
Ram Hill	53 F4
Rathbone Clo	53 E4
Rectory Rd	53 D1
Ridgeway	53 F2
Ridings Rd	53 E3
Robel Av	53 C1
Rockside Gdns	53 E1
Rose La	53 F3
Roundways	53 F3
Rushton Dri	53 F2
Ryecroft Rd	53 E1
Rylestone Clo	53 C1
St Annes Dri	53 F4
St Francis Rd	53 B3
St Michaels Clo	53 B2
St Peters Cres	53 E2
Salem Clo	53 C2
Sallys Way	53 B2
School Rd	53 B1
South View	53 E2
South View Cres	53 F3
South View Rise	53 F3
Stanford Rd	53 B1
Star Barn Rd	53 B2
Station Rd	53 E4
Sunnyside	53 E2
Swan La	53 A2
The Brake	53 E4
The Causeway	53 F2
The Close	53 E3
The Gully	53 C2
The Land	53 F2
The Orchard	53 E2
The Ridge	53 F2
The Ridings	53 E3
Thornhayes Clo	53 C1
Upper Chapel La	53 E2
Upper Stone Clo	53 F2
Vicarage Rd	53 E3
Watermore Clo	53 F2
Watleys End Rd	53 A2
Wayside Clo	53 E2
West Ridge	53 E2
Western Av	53 C1
Willow Way	53 F3
Winchcombe Rd	53 D1
Woodend Rd	53 E2
York Gdns	53 C2

WOTTON-UNDER-EDGE

Street	Ref
Adeys La	52 B4
Bear St	52 B5
Bearlands	52 B6
Beechwood Gro	52 D4
Blackquarries Hill	52 D4
Bradley Rd	52 A4
Bradley St	52 A4
Brickfields	52 B6
Browns Piece	52 B5
Cherry Orchard	52 C5
Chipping Clo	52 B5
Chipping Gdns	52 B5
Church St	52 C5
Church Walk	52 C5
Clarence Rd	52 B5
Coombe La	52 D4
Coombe Rd	52 C4
Cotswold Gdns	52 C5
Court Meadow	52 C5
Court Orchard	52 C5
Culverhay	52 B5
Dryleaze	52 A5
Dryleaze Ct	52 A5
Dryleaze Gdns	52 A5
Durns Rd	52 B5
Ellerncroft Rd	52 A4
Fountain Cres	52 C6
Gloucester Row	52 A4
Gloucester St	52 A4
Haw St	52 C6
Hentley Tor	52 C6
High St	52 B5
Hill Rd	52 C6
Holywell Rd	52 C4
Jays Mead	52 C5
Knapp Rd	52 C5
Lisle Pl	52 A4
Little Acre	52 A4
Locombe Pl	52 C6
Long St	52 B5
Ludgate Hill	52 B5
Manor La	52 C4
Market St	52 B5
Merlin Haven	52 A5
Mill Clo	52 C6
Mitre Pitch	52 C5
Mount Pleasant	52 C5
New Rd	52 A5
Oatground	52 C5
Old London Rd	52 A4
Old Town	52 B5
Orchard St	52 B5
Parkland	52 B4
Pitman Pl	52 C6
Potters Pond	52 B5
Queens Way	52 B5
Rope Walk	52 B5
Rosemary Ct	52 B5
School Rd	52 B5
Shepherds Leaze	52 B6
Shepherds Walk	52 C6
Symn La	52 B5
Synwell La	52 C5
Tabernacle Pitch	52 B4
Tabernacle Rd	52 B4
Tapscott Ct	52 A5
The Cloud	52 C5
Turnpike Av	52 C6
Valley Rd	52 C4
Venns Acre	52 B5
Water La	52 C5
West Vw	52 C5
Westfields	52 A5
Westridge Rd	52 A4
Wortley Rd	52 B5
Wortley Rd	52 C6
Wotton Cres	52 C6
Wotton Rd	52 A5

YATE/CHIPPING SODBURY

Street	Ref
Abbotswood	54 B6
Apperley Clo	54 B4
Argyle Dri	54 C1
Arnold Ct	55 F4
Badger Clo	54 B1
Badminton Rd	55 G5
Barnhill Rd	55 E3
Barnwood Rd	54 A5
Beaufort Av	54 A2
Beaufort Dri	54 A2
Birch Rd	54 B2
Birkdale	54 B4
Bisley	54 A5
Blaisdon	54 B6
Blanchards	55 G5
Blenheim Dri	54 A1
Bowling Hill	54 D3
Bowling La	55 E4
Brandash Rd	54 B6
Bredon	54 B6
Broad La	54 A1
Broad St	55 F4
Broad Way	54 D3
Brockworth	54 A6
Brook St	55 E3
Brookfield Clo	55 F3
Brookthorpe	54 A4
Burgage Clo	55 F4
Cabot Clo	54 D4
Cambrian Clo	54 B1
Cambrian Dri	54 B2
Canterbury Clo	54 C2
Carmarthan Clo	54 D1
Celestine Rd	54 A1
Cesson Clo	55 G4
Chalford Clo	54 B5
Chargrove	54 A5
Chatcombe	54 C5
Chatterton Rd	54 B3
Cherington	54 B6
Cherry Rd	54 D4
Cheshire Clo	54 B2
Chestnut Dri	55 E4
Chichester Way	54 B2
Church Farm Clo	54 C2
Church Rd	54 C1
Claypits Hill	54 D3
Cleeve Rd	54 B4
Colesbourne Clo	54 B5
Collett Way	54 A1
Cornwall Cres	54 D1
Cotswold Rd	55 E4
Court Dri	54 C4
Cranham	54 A5
Cranleigh Court Rd	54 B2
Crantock Rd	54 B3
Crowthers Av	54 C2
Culverhill Rd	55 E4
Deerhurst	54 A5
Doddington Rd	55 E5
Dorset Way	54 D2
Dovecote	54 C6
Downleaze Dri	55 E4
Dursley Clo	54 C4
*East Walk, North Walk	54 C3
Edgeworth	54 A6
Eggshill La	54 B3
Elm Clo	55 E4
Elmgrove Dri	54 C2
Elmhurst Gdns	54 D2
Elmore	54 A5
Elmwood	54 C4
Estoril	54 C4
Fairhaven	54 C4
Ferndown	54 C4
Finch Rd	54 D5
Fir Grove Cres	54 D2
Folly Bridge Clo	54 A3
Fox Av	54 B2
Frome Rd	55 F4
Gathorne Cres	54 B3
Gaunts Field	55 F5
Gaunts Rd	55 F5
Gleneagles	54 C4
Glenfall	54 B5
Goldcrest Rd	54 D5
Goose Green	54 A4
Goose Green Way	54 A1
Gorlands Rd	55 F3
Grace Clo	55 G3
Grassington Dri	54 C4
Gravel Hill	54 C1
Gravel Hill Rd	54 D1
Greenhayes	55 F5
Greenways Rd	54 A1
Gullivers Pl	55 E5
Halifax Rd	54 B1
Hampden Clo	54 B1
Hampshire Way	54 D1
Hardwick	54 A5
Harescombe	54 C5
Hartley Clo	55 G4
Hatherley	54 B5
Hatters La	55 F3
Heron Way	54 C5
High St	55 E4
Highfield Rd	54 D4
Highway	54 D3
Highworth Cres	54 B5
Homefield	54 C1
Home Orchard	54 B2
Horse St	55 F4
Horseshoe La	55 E4
Horton Rd	55 G2
Hounds Clo	55 F4
Hounds Rd	55 F4
Hoylake	54 C5
Jenner Clo	54 C4
Jubilee Gdns	55 E3
Kelston Clo	54 B6
Kenilworth	55 F4
Kennedy Way	54 B3
Kent Av	54 D1
Kestrel Clo	54 D5
Kingfisher Rd	54 D5
Kingrove Cres	55 F4
Kingrove La	55 F5
Kingscote	54 B6
Lancaster Rd	54 C1
Lansdown	54 A5
Lawns Rd	54 C3
Leaman Clo	55 E5
Lilliput Av	55 E5
Link Rd	54 C3
Littledean	54 C6
Longford	54 A5
Love La	55 E4
Lydbrook Clo	54 B5
Lyndale Rd	54 B3
Madison Clo	54 B2
Maisemore	54 B6
Mallard Clo	54 D4
Manor Way	55 F3
Maybank Rd	54 B3
Mead Rd	55 F4
Meadow Rd	54 D4
Melbourne Dri	55 F4
Melrose Av	54 D2
Melrose Rd	55 E3
Mercier Clo	54 D2
Merlin Way	54 D5
Meteor Clo	54 B1
Mill La	55 E3
Milton Clo	54 B3
Milton Rd	54 B3
Moordell Clo	54 A3
Moorland Rd	54 A3
Moorpark Av	54 A3
Mountbatten Clo	54 B1
Mow Barton	54 B3
Muirfield	54 C5
Nailsworth Av	54 B4
Newlyn Way	54 D3
*North Parade, Station Rd	54 C3
*North Walk, North Par	54 C3
Northfield	54 B5
Oak Clo	54 A1
Orchard Clo	54 C2
Painswick Clo	54 C4
Partridge Clo	54 D1
Piper Rd	54 C1
Pitchcombe	54 A5
Portway La	55 G3
Prescott	54 B5
Prestbury	54 B5
Priors Lea	54 B3
Quarry Rd	55 E3
Quedgeley	54 A5
Rectory Clo	54 C1
Ridgeway	54 D3
Ridings Clo	55 G4
River Rd	54 D4
Robin Way	54 D5
Rodborough	54 A6
Rodford Way	54 A5
Ross Clo	55 F3
Rounceval St	55 E4
St Andrews	54 C4
St Briavels Dri	54 A4
St Johns La	55 E3
St Johns Way	55 G3
St Marys Way	54 D2
Sandhurst	54 A5
School Walk	54 C3
Scott Way	54 C5
Shackleton Av	54 D4
Shire Way	54 A6
Shire Way	54 C5
Slimbridge	54 C6
Smarts Green	55 G5
Somerset Av	54 D2
*South Walk, Kennedy Way	54 C3
Spar Rd	54 B2
Stanshawe Cres	54 B3
Stanshawes Dri	54 B4
Staples Rd	54 B3
Station Clo	55 G5
Station Rd	54 A3
Stinchcombe	54 C4
Stirling Clo	54 B1
Streamside Rd	54 D4
Sturmer Clo	54 C1
Sundridge Park	54 C5
Sunningdale	54 C5
Sunnyside La	54 A3
Sutherland Av	54 B1
Templar Rd	54 C2
The Avenue	54 B3
The Glen	54 C2
The Leaze	54 B3
The Par	55 E4
The Willows	54 A3
Thorn Clo	54 B4
Thorn Farm	54 B3
Toddington Clo	54 B4
Treeleaze	54 C3
Troon	54 C5
Turnberry	54 C4
Two Stone La	55 F4
Turnpike Rd	54 C3
Tyndale Av	54 B2
Tyning Clo	54 C3
Ullswater Clo	54 C2
Vayre Clo	55 F3
Virginia Rd	54 D4
Walnut Av	54 D2
Walshe Av	55 G3
Waltonheath	54 C4
Warren Way	54 C2
Wellington Clo	54 B1
Wellington Dri	54 B1
Wellstead Av	54 B4
Wentworth	54 C4
*West Walk, North Walk	54 C3
Westerleigh Rd	54 A5
Westleigh Clo	54 A3
Whitcombe	54 A6
Whitefield	55 G4
Wickham Clo	55 G4
Wickwar Rd	55 E1
Wiltshire Av	54 D1
Windsor Dri	54 A2
Wistaria Av	54 D4
Woodchester	54 C6
Woodmancote	54 B8
Woodmans Clo	55 F4
Woodmans Rd	55 F4
Woodmans Vale	55 F4
York Clo	54 B1

YORKLEY

Street	Ref
Aisne Rd	56 F2
Ash Gro	56 E2
Bailey Hill	56 D2
Barn Cres	56 A3
Beech Rd	56 D1
Brierley Way	56 F2
Charleswood Rd	56 A3
Church Walk	56 F4
Corner Rd	56 B3
Crown La	56 C2
Cut & Fry Rd	56 E2
Danby Rd	56 E1
Deer Park	56 D2
George Rd	56 C1
Grove Rd	56 A3
Harold Rd	56 E1
Herberts Way	56 E3
High Delf Way	56 A3
Highview Rd	56 D1
Holly Tree Pl	56 F2
James Walk	56 B3
Johnsons Way	56 E1
Kidnalls Rd	56 B3
Link Rd	56 B1
Lower Rd	56 C1
Main Rd	56 B1
Morcroft Pl	56 C6
Morris Clo	56 E1
New Rd	56 B1
Oaklea Rd	56 D2
Oldcroft Rd	56 D1
Parkend Rd	56 D1
Phillips Clo	56 F1
Pillowell Rd	56 A1
Ridgeway	56 E1
St Swithins Rd	56 F1
School Rd	56 B1
Severn View Rd	56 E1
Shaphouse La	56 C1
Slade Rd	56 D1
Stagg Hill	56 C1
Stagg Hill Rd	56 C1
Tomlin Pl	56 E1
Tower Rd	56 D1
Tylers Way	56 E1
Upper Rd	56 B1
Wesley Rd	56 A1
Woodland Pl	56 E1
Yorkley La	56 B1
Yorkley Slade	56 E1
Yorkley Wood Rd	56 C1